Reducing Anger in Schools

This book provides school teachers, counselors, administrators, therapists, and parents an accessible and evidence-based approach to reduce violence in schools. The work outlines how self-esteem controls emotions and helps regulate expression of aggressive and violent feelings and behavior.

The work demonstrates in three distinct parts how faculty can reduce and prevent violence in their schools by using the student-teacher relationship: theory, case studies, and learning activities. Anger and violence are reduced through increasing children's self-esteem, which is developed through important relationships with adults.

The book invites teachers, school counselors, school psychologists, and other school administrators to rethink their relationships with children and to incorporate the relational ingredients needed to increase children's self-esteem by adopting features of evidence-based psychotherapy and demonstrating how such approaches can be applied in schools.

William Ketterer, PsyD, is a clinical psychologist. Currently, his focus is on psychological consultation and assisting schools in developing healing, relationship-based programming for troubled youth. He has a private practice in New Hampshire, USA.

Reducing Anger and Violence in Schools

An Evidence-Based Approach

William Ketterer, PsyD

**Contributions by
William Slammon, PhD
Krzysztof Bujarski, MD**

**Illustrations by
Matthew Greenway, MFA**

Routledge
Taylor & Francis Group

NEW YORK AND LONDON

First published 2020
by Routledge
52 Vanderbilt Avenue, New York, NY 10017

and by Routledge
2 Park Square, Milton Park, Abingdon, Oxon, OX14 4RN

Routledge is an imprint of the Taylor & Francis Group, an informa business

© 2020 Taylor & Francis

The right of William Ketterer to be identified as the author of this work has been asserted by him in accordance with sections 77 and 78 of the Copyright, Designs and Patents Act 1988.

Library of Congress Cataloging-in-Publication Data
A catalog record for this book has been requested

ISBN: 978-0-367-42780-1 (pbk)
ISBN: 978-0-367-42779-5 (hbk)
ISBN: 978-0-367-85504-8 (ebk)

Typeset in Bembo
by Apex CoVantage, LLC

For Will and Peter

Contents

Acknowledgements

I wish to thank the Blue Devils, Cadets, Cyclones, Engineers, Hurricanes, Raptors, Panthers, Royals, Marauders, Mustangs, Otters, Red Devils, Road Runners, Royals, Terriers, Tigers, Yellow Jackets, Wildcats, Wolves, Mice, Bears, Eagles, and Buffalo that roamed Sherwood's Village for providing me with a place to belong.

This work could not have been possible without the wisdom of Melissa Zoerheide, Steven Harper, Alex Bronner, Amanda Flodstrom, Christi Koch, Erica Young, Kim Moreno, Claire and Nathan Haskell, Elisabeth Parrott, Robert Eddy, Adrienne Abbot, Emily Leopold, Sarah Zwikelmaier, Kate Leech, Patricia Song, Rebecca Walter, Athur Maerlender, Colby Smith, Theodore Ellenhorn, Ryan Kuehlthau, Tom Gamble, Mary Schneider, David Drazin, Raymond Chin, Debra Lopez, Skye Payne, Tony Robinson, Vance Sherwood, Larry Brown, Carla McCall, Melvin Miller, Polly Young-Eisendrath, Richard Geist, Melinda Haas, and Jeff Slavin.

I thank both the Waban, Massachusetts and the Sharon, Vermont reading groups for helping me understand and apply the ideas of Heinz Kohut, and for encouraging me to use them in novel ways.

I am indebted to the good people of the White River Valley Supervisory Union for their encouragement for this project. Specifically, I thank Deb Matthews and Bruce Labs.

Finally, and most importantly, Hollie, for your endless encouragement and for our bicycle rides where we thought through these ideas together, thanks.

Introduction

Fishing With Grant

Grant entered preschool at age four. He had essentially been abandoned at birth and was being raised by loving, older caregivers. Grant yelled profanity, punched, kicked, and bit students and teachers. He flung chairs and ripped up papers. He would be sent to the office, then sent home. Each new day was just like the last. Teachers and administrators had to physically restrain him to keep him and others safe. When he was calm, Grant's smile lit up the room, but everyone's hearts broke when he went berserk. Other students quickly learned to stay clear of Grant and his anger. Although small for his age, Grant's rage held the entire school hostage.

To help Grant, his school created a positive reward system to give him an incentive for pro-social behavior. They also implemented a check-in and checkout system, provided a safe person to whom he could tell his feelings at the start and end of each day, and increased the staffing at the preschool. School staff explained these new procedures to Grant. They asked that he draw pictures of his feelings and make positive behavioral choices. They taught him strategies, like how to take three deep breaths when he was upset, and provided him a time-away space to cool off. Nothing worked.

After the initial first few weeks of school and all the turmoil he was experiencing and causing others, his preschool teacher, Melanie, discovered the one thing that Grant enjoyed: fishing. Grant loved to fish. It didn't matter what type of fish or how . . . fishing was it.

Melanie became especially interested in Grant and his love of fishing. Sitting with him, she attempted to understand what fishing meant to him and why he obsessed over it. Melanie didn't judge it as "good" or "bad," but wanted to understand its significance for this troubled little child.

Having been introduced to the ideas in *Reducing Anger and Violence in Schools,* Melanie wanted to give the concepts within the book a try. Rather than demanding that Grant engage with his peers or stop talking about fishing, Melanie pulled him aside and listened. She listened with her heart for both what he was verbalizing and what he wasn't saying with words, all the while paying close attention to her own thoughts, feelings, and reactions.

Melanie hypothesized that Grant wasn't really fishing for fish—maybe fishing, she thought, was really about finding his birth parents and also about being a big boy and taking care of himself. Fishing for Grant represented both a tragic story of loss and a longing for maturity. Whenever he talked about catching "the big one" that got away in the end, Melanie imagined that he was really talking about not getting to know his family. Deeply connected to her own family, Melanie began to try to imagine what it was like for Grant. She tried to feel, think, and sense as Grant and to let go of her own identity . . . to walk in Grant's shoes. After a while, Grant began to hit others at school a little less.

Nearing the winter break, Grant started hitting again. This setback coincided with a distinct rupture in his family and home life. Once again, Melanie sat with Grant as he raged and listened for what he was trying to communicate. She did her best to offer an empathic connection and response. Melanie organized her day so she could spend more time one-on-one with Grant. She soon realized that Grant didn't know who was really in charge of him at home or at school. Moreover, just as Grant didn't really know who was in charge, neither did the school! Was the principal, assistant principal, special educator, case manager, teacher support person, therapist, or the teacher responsible for him at school?

In addition, Melanie thought her classroom structure was too loose and decided to take better control of it. Her students began walking in line to the cafeteria and word in the classroom was that Melanie was to be obeyed. She readily volunteered to be fully responsible for Grant. Melanie was in command! Grant's education, behavior difficulties, and discipline rested on her shoulders. She read psychology texts, attended conferences, and found meaning in her new responsibilities. She was determined to be a teacher who taught the student, not the subject.

As Melanie and Grant became closer, his hostility waned. He was able to sit in circle, sing, and learn his letters. Grant now spent the entire day in the preschool. He followed the rules, made friends, and no longer punched and kicked as much. Although he continued to love fishing, the intensity of his obsession diminished. His peers forgave him and began including him in their play. He laughed and smiled more often.

Discussion

Melanie's relationship with Grant was in itself healing. Her thoughtful care was the cure. Melanie was able to use her relationship with Grant to invite him to be known, to trust her, to stop using violence to be heard, and to get to the hard work of learning.

When children sense that their self-worth is challenged or threatened, they become angry and may behave violently, just as Grant did. Many teachers, parents, and students are becoming more concerned with violence in schools and what they can do to address it. Understanding, and ultimately reducing, school violence is a top priority for many schools and communities and is precisely why the information found in *Reducing Anger and Violence in Schools* on how to treat violent, aggressive behavior in troubled children is so timely and relevant for educators today.

The Healing the Self approach explored in this book is based on the perhaps surprising finding that such anger and violence provide a temporary feeling of wholeness or a "replacement" for durable, authentic self-esteem. Anger, then, is an attempt by the mind to compensate for the lack of a fundamental sense of self-worth. Under anger is pain that self-esteem can help children manage. The Healing the Self model outlined herein teaches that when the teacher, parent, or therapist provide an admirable role model, such as Melanie did for Grant, and use reliable structure, recognize the pain the child feels, and create a sense of belonging, the child can learn to better manage their own feelings and behavior.

Children develop authentic, lasting self-esteem through special relationships with adults (Elson, 1987). Although relationships with other children often play an important role in the development of a child's self-esteem, there is no substitute for what special relationships with adults contribute to this critical piece of development. When adults increase a child's self-esteem, both anger and violence are reduced.

Adults who work with children know the power of the relationship. Just as Melanie discovered in working with Grant, they know relationships have the potential to help or hurt. Research shows violence can be prevented through relationships and that it is the relationship itself that is the intervention which leads to growth and reduces anger (Wexler, 1999). *Reducing Anger and Violence in Schools* focuses on how strong relationships are necessary for children to develop and maintain their self-esteem. It provides teachers, therapists, school counselors, and other adults a way of understanding how to better connect and ultimately help kids feel less angry, behave less violently, and improve their sense of self-worth.

This book teaches the relational ingredients that encourage children to be pro-social, happy, and regulate their emotions. It demonstrates how adults can strengthen their relationships with children. It's intended to serve as an invitation to adults to consider the importance of their relationships with kids and how to best cultivate a positive, strong connection with them. All children need caring, thoughtful adults to engage with them and help them grow.

To create self-esteem we must start by understanding it and identifying the core components—the interpersonal experiences—that come together to enable children to feel their feelings without falling apart, becoming overwhelmed by anger, or behaving aggressively. The Healing the Self model suggests that, for children to grow, they require relationships with adults that have three key ingredients:

- Healthy idealization
- Empathic attunement
- A sense of belonging

By understanding these key ingredients, care providers can share a common language as they work to develop strategies that can help children. *Reducing Anger and Violence in Schools* explores each of these three interrelated ingredients, outlines specific approaches teachers and clinicians can use to meet them, and provides learning activities designed to allow these adults to better understand and more effectually apply these concepts.

The Healing the Self approach teaches a method for increasing self-esteem that is research-driven and practice-informed. It adopts features of evidence-based psychotherapy and demonstrates how such approaches can be applied in schools. The model comes from more than twenty years of experience the author has had in assisting and witnessing young people reduce violence and anger through increasing their self-esteem. Derived from multiple theoretical perspectives regarding violence, this book is an attempt to make the ideas in *Reducing Anger and Violence in Schools* usable in a real-world setting by people who care about children.

Teachers, therapists, mentors, and school counselors can provide children with the necessary ingredients to build and maintain self-esteem through their school-based relationships. *Reducing Anger and Violence in Schools* provides a framework for teachers and others to apply evidence-based, psychotherapeutically derived skills and concepts to the classroom in a model that is straightforward to learn and apply.

The work is organized into informational sections, each followed by a case study and learning activities. Case studies elucidate the principles in each chapter and strive to be both scientific and human. Identifying information has been altered and quotations are from non-verbatim transcripts.

References

Elson, M. (1987). *The Kohut seminars: On self psychology with adolescents and young adults.* New York, NY: W.W. Norton and Company.

Wexler, D. M. (1999). The broken mirror: A self psychological treatment perspective for relationship violence. *The Journal of Psychotherapy Practice and Research*, 8(2): 129–141.

1 Healing the Self Model

As noted in the Introduction, the Healing the Self model can be a powerful way to deal with anger and violence in children with low self-esteem through the formation of meaningful relationships with educators and caregivers. The model suggests that because children develop through relationships, the relationship itself is the intervention for aggressive behavior; what adults do specifically in their efforts to help children control their behavior isn't as important as their ability to connect with the child in a meaningful way.

Teaching educators and other caregivers how to meaningfully relate to aggressive and violent children is the foundation of the Healing the Self model. The approach is based on the assumption that relationships need not be traditionally "therapeutic" to help children—teachers, mentors, principals, and others can provide children with the necessary ingredients to build and maintain self-esteem through their school-based relationships. The Healing the Self model introduces evidence-based therapeutic approaches to non-therapists demonstrating how to:

- Establish themselves as an admirable role model
- Take an empathic stance with children
- Create a sense of belonging

The Three Relational Components of the Healing the Self Model

Research shows that children's self-esteem is not based on their aptitude, abilities, or their current mood, but instead is a direct result of their relationships with important people in their lives. Typically, these relational needs are met in early childhood, and as the child matures and enters school, the foundation is laid for them to psychologically expand their capacity for relationships with others. For some children, however, these needs, sometimes despite the good intentions of adults, are not met. When this occurs, many children behave in ways that demand the attention of teachers, therapists, and other adults in an ultimate effort to drive the primary caregivers in the child's life to meet those needs.

Educational and clinical experiences suggest that good teachers and therapists naturally try to meet their students' and clients' emotional needs. However, as the Healing the Self model teaches, in order for a relationship to help a child heal from developmental gaps, restore or build self-esteem, and reduce the expression of anger and violence, it must include three ingredients:

- Idealization
- Empathy
- Belonging

By understanding and applying these core ingredients to relationships, care providers can share a common language as they work to develop strategies that can help children. In the next three chapters, we will explore each of these three interrelated ingredients in greater detail. Learning activities designed to allow adults to better understand and more effectually apply these concepts will also be presented within these chapters.

Commonly Accepted Definition of Self-Esteem

Self-esteem is important, foundational, and necessary for children to control their emotions and their behaviors. But what is it? How and why does it support emotional stability? And what can teachers, therapists, childcare providers, and parents do to help children develop it?

Self-esteem is generally considered synonymous with how someone feels about himself or herself. According to the Mayo Clinic, "Self-esteem is shaped by your thoughts, relationships, and experiences" (Mayo Staff, 2014). Self-esteem can involve a variety of beliefs about the self, such as the appraisal of one's own appearance, emotions, and abilities. Self-esteem is also important because it lays the foundation for how a person treats others and allows others to treat them.

Expanded Definition of Self-Esteem

Rather than thinking of self-esteem as primarily someone's appraisal of his or her own ability, research has expanded the notion of self-esteem to encompass the broader idea of a sense of self. In general parlance, the term describes a person's sense of self-worth. But self-esteem isn't simply how people view themselves—it is the vantage point from which they view themselves, others, and everything around them. It is a person's main driving force. Most people have a cohesive, enduring, internal core that allows them to understand themselves, others, and reality, and this can be considered as their sense of self (Ornstein, 1998).

Although technically difficult to define, self-esteem is a theoretical construct that is used to conceptualize many enduring personality traits.

Self-esteem also serves to attract people who are similar. Moreover, most people are never psychologically alone, because in their minds they have internalized the traits of many others. In the case of children, self-esteem is what enables a child to appropriately feel emotions, control behavior, and make friends.

Children have specific psychological needs, including the need to admire other people, although this need changes over time. Children also need people to validate their construction of reality and they need to belong. This need to belong drives them to make friends and associate with other people whom they can experience as similar to themselves. When these needs are met, the relationships and interactions that fostered them are absorbed into the person's personality or self (Socarides & Stolorow, 1985). In this sense, having a healthy self requires other people.

A sense of self or this expanded "self-esteem" is gained through relationships. This occurs most commonly in childhood through the relationship with the parent(s). Typically, children admire their parents and experience their parents as being like them. Parents validate the child's experience and thus the parent and child feel deeply connected. In the child's mind, this mixture of sameness, admiration, and connection generates feelings of security, self-worth, and confident aspiration (i.e., self-esteem). "If mom loves me," the child thinks, "I must be lovable."

But it can sometimes be very difficult to understand exactly what a child needs in order to feel connected to important adults in their life because children, especially young ones, live in a fantasy world. Children base their emotions on their imagination. One only needs to ask a preschooler if she rode a dinosaur to school and receive a smiling "Yes" to confirm that adults and children do not occupy the same reality. Children live in the world of pretend. Ultimately, meeting a child's psychological needs requires entering that pretend world. Unfortunately, of course, some children's needs are completely unmet—or worse—because adults are unable to enter this world.

Figure 1.1

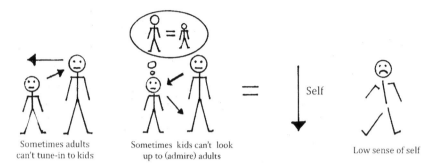

Sometimes adults
can't tune-in to kids

Sometimes kids can't look
up to (admire) adults

Self

Low sense of self

Figure 1.2

Caregivers may believe they are meeting a child's needs, but if in the child's mind the unspoken need isn't met, it isn't met. Although no one is at fault, the child may have deficits in his or her sense of self.

Understanding the Anger/Violence/Self-Esteem Trio

When a child's psychological needs are not met, anger and violence are often the result. Anger and violence are directly related to self-esteem (Donnellan, Trzesniewski, Robins, Moffitt, & Caspi, 2005). The American Psychological Association generally considers anger an emotion children have when they feel they have been wronged or misunderstood. Anger is a feeling that children experience in their minds and bodies. They may sweat and have an increased heart rate. The may feel hot, dizzy, have a stomach ache, or exhibit any number of physical signs. In its most basic sense, anger is a feeling.

Violence or aggression, on the other hand, is a behavior. It is an action intended to harm another. Although seemingly similar to assertiveness, aggression differs in important ways. Anna Ornstein, an internationally known psychiatrist, explains that the foundations of aggression are feelings of "fear, distress and hostility; [w]hereas the foundation of assertiveness is feelings of joy, interest, and excitement" (Ornstein, 1998, p. 55). Although easy to confuse, at its root aggression is very different from assertiveness. Most childhood aggression is out of anger (Family Life Development Center, 2001). Anger is the feeling that causes most children, and many adults for that matter, to behave aggressively. Anger is the emotional fuel for aggression. Aggression differs from anger, because it's not a feeling—it's a behavior. A child feels angry but behaves aggressively.

Healing the Self Case Study: I'm a Soldier

David was a 10-year-old boy who read well and loved math. He was active and very well-spoken. Intellectually, he was way ahead of his peers. David, however, suffered in a world populated with grown-ups that didn't behave well. Family illness, finances, relational difficulties, legal troubles, and substance abuse issues made his home a battle ground. Further complicating matters was the fact that the community was well aware of his family's struggles. David refused to engage with peers, complete school work, or participate. He had no friends, isolated himself, and when he wasn't yelling, he kept to himself with head hung down. When he did talk, he screamed "I'm angry," and when invited to process, told complex, exaggerated tales that emphasized his intellect, power, or specialness. David told tall tales and adamantly reminded everyone that in the second grade he had been a soldier and was very dangerous. He didn't let anyone know the real David, just the super tough, false, phony David.

Faculty wondered if his tales of grandeur were his best attempt at hiding both himself and a deep sense of shame that alienated him. His teachers focused on empathizing with David regarding the meaning of his stories, rather than proving he was wrong, and playfully joined him in his story telling. Of course David hadn't walked on the moon, but what did his stories mean? David's teachers agreed to use the Healing the Self model and refrained from challenging his stories. They attempted to deeply understand him. Maybe David felt scared, vulnerable, and boring, so identifying with being a soldier made him feel brave, tough, and exciting. Faculty developed the plan that whenever David needed to talk, he could step away and check in with the co-teacher, Lars. As long as he completed his academic responsibilities, David could talk to Lars. Lars decided that rather than convince David that he was brave, tough, and exciting or to focus on simply rewarding any on-task behavior, he would listen carefully to David's stories and try to imagine their meaning with David. Then, Lars would join David in his imaginative play.

David told Lars of afternoon firefights with the Taliban in Afghanistan, out-swimming sharks in the Indian Ocean, jumping out of helicopters over Borneo, and raiding a den of thieves in Morocco. Lars hypothesized that David really, really needed an interested adult who had the capacity to feel with him. Lars never told David, "You must be hurting, so telling me these phony stories makes you tough," or "You want me to know how smart you are because you know all these exotic places." Instead, Lars allowed himself to play along with David. First thing in the morning, when David reported that he single-handedly sunk a pirate ship off the Libyan coast, Lars responded with, "Awesome, way to go Captain, I knew you could," or "You must be exhausted. Wow! What an adventure!" Lars both authentically joined David in his play and seemed to genuinely look forward to his creative stories.

David's adventures slowly changed. From the battles where everyone but David usually died, to racing Ferraris, summiting Mt. Everest, and piloting a hot air balloon, his tales became less murderous and death-defying. At the same time, David began playing with other children during recess. He showed classmates vulnerability when he told them he wasn't very good at kickball. Lars saw David make friends and engage in cooperative play. David also confided in Lars some of his real insecurities, and even told classmates that he sometimes worried about his family.

As Lars worked with David the two became a team. It was clear to everyone that David looked up to Lars and the two of them had a special language. Given time, David was able to generalize his relationship with Lars to his other teacher, Rachel, and eventually to peers. By Lars engaging with David, he communicated that David was worthy. He didn't have to lie to be special; he was special because Lars was cool and Lars liked him. David appeared happier and slowly allowed others to see the real David. When David revealed his true self, inadequacies and all, Lars and Rachel wondered if it meant that he had tamed some of the sense of shame that had ruled him.

Discussion

As of this writing, David appears far less angry and is able to complete school work independently for much of the day. He has developed age-appropriate, pro-social friendships with peers. When frustrated, he can self-advocate and calm himself down. David still relies on his powerful imagination to insulate himself from difficult feelings, but his academics are strong and he no longer screams. David's relationship with Lars provided him with the idealization, empathy, and sense of belonging he needed to feel wanted and ultimately increase his self-esteem.

Self-esteem is the psychological strength that allows the child to feel anger without "doing" anger by behaving violently. The difference between a child having the capacity to feel a terrible feeling and do something terrible is vital. Current research suggests that self-esteem is the very construct that enables us to access our emotional worlds while at the same time empowering us to inhibit bad, aggressive, or self-destructive behaviors (Donnellan, Trzesniewski, Robins, Moffitt, & Caspi, 2015).

Most parents and teachers naturally strive to meet children's relational needs and assist them in this development. However, because some children may not have had the experience of others meeting their needs, they may not have an internal model that allows them to readily accept a caring adult's attempts to help them. In fact, children may go to great lengths to prevent the feared letdown of adults not meeting their needs (Ornstein, 1981). In such circumstances, it is up to the adult to creatively undertake the challenge of supporting self-esteem development and supply the tools needed to help effectively. Through educating teachers, therapists, and childcare providers on how to create close, healing connections, the Healing the Self model provides a straightforward way to raise self-esteem, reduce both anger and violence, and assist in constructing a healthier sense of self.

In Chapter 2, we explore the concept of Idealization as taught by the Healing the Self model. Establishing themselves as an admirable role model that children can idealize is the first way caring adults can create healthy, connected relationships with children who suffer with poor self-worth.

References

Donnellan, M. B., Trzesniewski, K. H., Robins, W. R., Moffitt, E. T., & Caspi, A. (2015). Low self-esteem is related to aggression, antisocial behavior and delinquency. *American Psychological Society, 16*(4), 328–335.

Family Life Development Center. (2001). *Therapeutic crisis intervention: A crisis prevention and management System.* Ithaca, NY: Cornell University Press.

Mayo Clinic Staff. (2014). *Ranges of self-esteem, healthy life style: Adult health.* Retrieved from http://www.mayoclinic.org/healthy-lifestyle/adult-health/in-depth/self-esteem.

Ornstein, A. (1981). Self-pathology in childhood: Developmental and clinical considerations. *Psychiatric Clinics of North America, 4*(3), 435–453.

Ornstein, A. (1998). The fate of narcissistic rage in psychotherapy. *Psychoanalytic Inquiry, 18*(1), 55–70.

Socarides, D. D., & Stolorow, R. D. (1985). Affects and self objects. In D. Terman (Ed.), *The self and the Oedipus complex* (pp. 105–119). New York, NY: International Universities Press.

2 Idealization

The Healing the Self model teaches that in order for children to overcome angry, aggressive behavior brought on by a lack of self-esteem that comes from not having their needs met, they must have meaningful relationships with adults. The Healing the Self approach asserts that if that relationship is going to help a child heal from developmental gaps it must include idealization, empathy, and belonging.

Establishing oneself as an admirable role model that children can idealize is the first way a caring adult can create healthy, connected relationships with children who suffer with poor self-worth. In this chapter we will discuss this idealization component in greater detail, outlining how a strong, structured relationship that is based on authenticity enables children to idealize important adults in their life.

Why Idealization Is Important

Idealization is a critical early ingredient for development of the self. A child must idealize and wish to mesh with their caregiver in order to develop a psychological core. Most children naturally admire the adults in their lives. Two examples may clarify this point. The first occurs when a newborn baby cries. In that moment, many believe the child seeks to have a strong connection with the parent. They may wish to merge with the responsive parent they believe they control by crying—the child then begins to idealize the caregiver's power to soothe them.

The second example comes from Richard Geist, EdD, of the Harvard Medical School. In an advanced seminar for therapists, Dr. Geist asked the therapists to consider idealizing behavior this way: Imagine a toddler falling and scratching his knee. The boy screams, "Mommy!" Mother runs over and comforts him with a kiss on the knee. The kiss instantly heals the injury, and moments later the child is happily playing. In the child's mind the kiss truly "healed" the injury. This is because of the child's idealization of the mother. A kiss from someone else might have no effect because, in the child's mind, the mother is endowed with special powers. These special powers are the result of the child's idealization of their mother.

Figure 2.1

Figure 2.2

Idealization is also seen in teenagers who may plaster their bedroom walls with posters of celebrities. The teenager may be longing to merge with an idealized other.

In essence, idealization can be understood as an external representation of a person's internal psychic world. An idealized world eventually becomes less idealized as the child matures. This is because as children grow into adults, the need to idealize others recedes to become a lingering relationship stage rather than a relationship's defining characteristic.

No one could fall in love without first idealizing the other. Idealization is an initial phase in the development of mature relationships. Healthy adults learn to manage the idealization as they come to terms with the imperfections of a beloved partner. Conversely, divorce can be understood as the total abandonment of our idealized view of a spouse, who may then be completely un-idealized.

As children mature, they typically begin to look up to others and to aspects of themselves. They can idealize parts of themselves on the inside rather than always needing to look for idealization on the outside. These are the good feelings people have when they behave responsibly.

This concept of self-idealization can be better understood through the, arguably counter-culture, children's song "Puff the Magic Dragon," in which the whimsical character of Puff adventures with Jackie Paper. When Jackie is no longer a boy, he no longer needs Puff. As a child matures, he or she outgrows the need to idealize important adults but retains the secure sense

Figure 2.3

of self nurtured by that idealization. The child, in a sense, internalizes the idealized relationship. If idealization needs are met in childhood, then as the child matures, adults no longer need to be all-powerful and all-knowing and can become real people.

Unfortunately, when people continue to need to idealize others into late adolescence and adulthood it can mean that the person is scared of part of themselves. Excessive idealization exercised by adults forecloses authentic relationships, effectively erecting walls of non-reality rather than bringing individuals closer. When adults idealize other adults it can be problematic for both. To explain this phenomenon, think of the idealization that occurs between performers and fans who may adore each other in concept, but freeze in discomfort should they meet in-person. Idealization prevents an authentic relationship because both parties actually occupy somewhat depersonalized roles, rather than revealing their true selves in the imperfection that is closeness.

Thus, as is the case for so many tools of psychological development, idealization is a method that has its time and place and must be used so that it can be discarded. For instance, idealization is healthy when adults idealize a code of conduct, but idealization can be unhealthy when it inhibits relationships.

Fostering Idealization

There are many ways of helping children idealize adults. Children may admire adults for their knowledge, athleticism, artistic talent, or any number of other abilities. Idealization can also be created from the outside through **structuring** the encounter, and it can occur from the inside when the child senses that the adult can handle their own feelings. In this way the adult can be real, or, in other words, **authentic**.

Structuring

One way of helping a student idealize adults is by structuring the relationship and defining clear expectations. This often helps the child admire the adult because it communicates that the grown-up is strong enough to handle the child's behaviors and emotions. By structuring the encounter, the adult communicates that they are competent, can stay in reality, and are worthy of respect.

Let's return to the story of Grant that was highlighted in the Introduction for a real-world example of how structuring can help children idealize adults. In Grant's case, Melanie had begun forming a close, connected relationship with him that was helping him sort through his big emotions and had been somewhat effective in curbing his aggressive behavior. However, Grant was still hitting and often did not feel as if anyone was in charge of him at home or at school. Melanie realized she needed to take better charge of her classroom in an effort to help Grant gain control of his emotions. By taking command, she communicated to Grant that she had the resolve and character strength not only to care for him, but also to hold and understand his inner emotional world. Melanie's classroom became a tight ship and she demanded that her students straighten up and act right on her ship. By doing so, she increased the value of her empathic stance. She wasn't trying to understand Grant out of fear of his emotions or behaviors, but out of genuine, caring concern for him. This allowed Grant to open up to her and idealize her as both a leader in his world and a nurturing caregiver. This idealization enabled Grant to feel safe enough to trust Melanie and allow her to know the real him.

Teachers can employ the same process that Melanie did by providing students with clear expectations of conduct and responsibilities. Using class scheduling and adhering to it provides students with a predictable and consistent classroom. Often, children who believe that important others can't handle their feelings require very consistent structure to convince them that adults are capable of emotionally caring for them. In therapy training, this structure in the relationship comes about when therapists "hold the therapeutic frame." This includes starting and stopping sessions on time, respecting confidentiality, and requiring payment, as well as the other parameters of a therapeutic encounter.

Authenticity

Authenticity is another way that idealization can be formed in relationships, and is vital from a relational perspective. Artificial slogans and canned verbal interventions such as therapeutic "scripts," while conceptually valuable, most often fail (McWilliams, 2004). Authentic, "idealizable" adult behavior must rely instead on the adults' own judgment and their ability to select the best language interventions in the moment.

In addition, complimenting children with a poor sense of self rarely helps them. The child needs to idealize the adult and, if the adult praises mediocre work in an effort to help the child feel well, it backfires. Compliments, praise, encouragement, or similarly well-intentioned words may actually prevent idealization; if the adult compliments something that is average as if it is outstanding, then the adult is a fool. And why admire a fool? True praise or validation, however, is very important and will be discussed in greater detail in Chapter 3.

Sometimes adults get it backwards and idealize the child. They look up to the child and want the child to overly validate them. The well-known therapist and feminist thinker Polly Young-Eisendrath warns that big problems can occur when this happens (Young-Eisendrath, 2008). Children want to know that caregivers are up to the task of meeting their needs and handling their feelings. "After all, if the grown-ups can't handle their own emotions, how on Earth can they handle mine?" the child reasons.

Carl Rogers, MD, discovered that people who are suffering terribly from their inner emotional worlds can readily sense when others aren't being authentic with them. Children with a low sense of self know when adults around them seem phony. This is because they are looking to adults to care for them and may be worried that the grown-ups can't, so they test them. Therefore, taking honest stock of one's own authenticity is vital to the process of building a meaningful relationship with children. Of course, not all adults can build meaningful relationships with all children. Luckily, they don't have to. Children can benefit from a strong relationship with a single adult to help him or her mature. In schools and clinics, encouraging faculty authenticity can be done by scheduling a regular time in the day or week where staff are invited to talk openly to other adults about their experiences with a child to ensure that each care provider is adequately supported.

Idealization Case Study: Pie's Climb

Pie was a high school student who came from an intact, middle class, professional family. Although bright, he had a type of visual neglect learning disability that prevented him from seeing details in his writing, such as commas or even certain words. He loved ideas and reading, but couldn't pass simple tests or even write an email without feeling stupid and misunderstood. Pie was angry, and he lived in turmoil.

On the outside, Pie was dashing. Although handsome on the outside, on the inside Pie felt terrible. People often thought that Pie was angry, but deep inside he was sad.

Pie rarely attended school. Instead, he visited museums, read by himself, or fly fished at a local creek. His high school was concerned about his many absences. His teachers gave him a point system for attending school, and a counselor was assigned to him; he even had a special support class to help him get through the day. But Pie hated it all. He said terrible things like, "School is where mindless gorillas grunt nothingness," or "There is no way that spending the day in a museum isn't a better education than this public high school."

Mental health therapy failed. Pie told his therapist that by her declaring to him how he felt, she was living in her own imagination. "It's actually impossible for you to know how I'm feeling, you don't know me," he repeated. Deep down, he believed that counseling was about submission, control, and the therapist thinking he or she was somehow better than he was. Pie went to many therapists, but it all ended the same way—he wasn't able to benefit from counseling. Eventually, Pie's behavior deteriorated and his parents enrolled him in a smaller, private boarding school.

One of Pie's teachers at the new school was a brilliant, well-read man named Rob. Besides having read the same books as Pie, Rob was an avid rock climber, something that Pie greatly admired. Pie felt he had found a real teacher at last. He and his friends played a game with Rob where they tried to stump him. Students could ask Rob anything, and he would answer any question they threw at him. Rob nearly always won.

Rob brought climbing magazines to the school and showed rock climbing videos. Pie became fascinated with the sport and Rob literally showed him the ropes, explaining that it didn't matter what you said or thought, gravity never turned off—he had to train hard and dial in your focus. Rob assured Pie, however, that if worked hard he could handle even the most difficult routes. He taught Pie that if you fell you fell, and success or failure depended on your strength and creativity. At the same time, Rob listened to Pie and tried his best to understand how crummy it felt to be imprisoned by a learning disability. Rob was strict, but Pie cared for him deeply. Rob helped Pie believe in himself. Rob was an authentic person; he spoke openly and honestly with Pie. He didn't treat Pie as an equal, but as a student. Pie opened up to Rob, but Rob didn't tell Pie his history or his problems. When Rob was with Pie, it was Rob's job to be his teacher, and Pie's job to be himself.

Eventually Pie received the type of writing help that he needed and began to love school. Rob introduced Pie to thinkers like Plato, Aristotle, Tolstoy, Marx, and Kant. Pie beamed joyfully when he explained *The Critique of Pure Reason* to his teacher over lunch in the cafeteria. One day, before Pie graduated, Rob confided, "Pie, it used to be really difficult to be around you, but now I like spending time with you." Years later, Pie and Rob climbed together as equals.

Discussion

The reason Pie had never excelled prior to attending his new school is that he didn't idealize his teachers or previous therapists. The harder they tried to help him, the more alone and distraught he became. Pie thought that by helping him they were communicating that they were better than him. When Pie met Rob, however, he found someone he could look up to. Rob was book smart and knew how to rock climb—something that Pie found worthy of respect. Through this form of idealization, Pie was able to start the process of believing in himself. Rob deeply impacted Pie. After graduation, he enrolled in a community college and eventually earned a four-year college degree.

It is important to see the value of idealization in building a healthy, stable sense of self. Educators, mentors, and parents must establish themselves as an admirable role model that children can look up to. Initially, children must idealize care providers, but if the need to idealize is met, idealization naturally diminishes as the child matures. In the next chapter, we will examine why empathy is the next step to building meaningful relationships with children who may be suffering with low self-worth.

Learning Activities

Think of the adults you admired as a child. Write down the traits you admired about them.

1.   Are these traits that you admire today?
2.   How did the people you idealized handle their feelings?
3.   Why was the relationship with the idealized adult important?
4.   How did the nature of the relationship change as you matured?

Application Activity

Think of the children you work with. Do any of them admire you? Make a list of the students who might idealize you and write down why. Not every child can idealize every adult. List the struggling students. Do they admire you? Why or why not?

References

McWilliams, N. (2004). *Psychoanalytic psychotherapy: A practitioner's guide.* New York, NY: Guilford Press.

Young-Eisendraft, P. (2008). *The self-esteem trap: Raising confident and compassionate kids in an age of self-importance.* New York, NY: Little, Brown and Company.

3   Empathy

In Chapter 2, we established the importance of setting oneself up as an admirable role model in order to begin creating a healthy sense of self in children who struggle with emotional problems. This is the first step in implementing the Healing the Self model. The next step in building meaningful relationships is to learn how to empathize with a child struggling to control their behavior. Empathy is a vital ingredient in increasing self-esteem in such children. To build self-worth, adults must empathize with children, but empathy can be easily misunderstood.

Empathy is often confused with sympathy. Sympathy is feeling for someone, whereas empathy is taking another's perspective, which can be done without any feeling of nurturance. A rather macabre example can be found in the Germans' treatment of the British during World War II. The Nazis used empathy to imagine ways to further terrorize the citizens of London by adding sirens to bombs to increase their victims' sense of chaos and fear. In this way, they took on the Londoners' perspective, clearly showing an empathic attunement with the British that had absolutely nothing whatsoever to do with having any sympathy for them.

Taking and understanding someone else's perspective, as we do when we are being empathetic, doesn't necessarily mean agreeing with them. When a child wails because he wants a second bowl of ice cream, understanding his perspective doesn't mean giving in to the demand and, for example, scooping another bowl. Acquiescing can communicate that the adult can't handle the child's frustration and can therefore impede healthy idealization. Instead, empathy can be employed to help understand how special the ice cream is to the child and therefore the reason for the child's feelings.

The personality theorist and world-renowned neurologist Heinz Kohut, MD, believed that empathy is so important to children and adults that when important people do not empathize with us, it is traumatizing (Kohut, 1957). People can even feel let down when a stranger doesn't empathize with them. A simple example of this is when we smile at someone and they do not smile back. Do we not feel slightly annoyed when the recipient of our kind gesture doesn't return the favor?

When people who are important to us do not understand our perspective, it is not only a tremendous letdown, but also incredibly frustrating. Children need adults to be able to understand their perspective and to validate their reality so that they can learn to trust what they know and how they see the world. Very young children need adults to be empathically attuned to them in order to help them organize and define their emotional experiences. Empathy is a necessary building block in a child's development of their own mind.

One way of understanding empathy is as a means of data collection—one that is helpful for both the information gleaned and the investment inherent in such an activity (Bacal, 1985). By imagining the child's inner world, caregivers are able to hypothesize about the child's experience. This is not to say that the therapist's or teacher's guesses are all or even mostly correct. Rather, the real value of the empathic approach is that the adult's effort to understand provides an avenue for increased emotional investment and emotional closeness.

The case history of Melanie and Grant introduced at the beginning of the book is a good example of this. Melanie spent some time observing Grant and his love of fishing to hypothesize about Grant's experience. She spent time "collecting data" about Grant and what his obsession with fishing might be about and tried to determine where the gaps in his family dynamic might be that caused Grant so much trouble. To help him, Melanie had to let go of her own way of understanding family. She had to step out of herself and imagine what it would be like for Grant, to empathize with Grant. She had always liked school, but had to try to feel like Grant to understand how school—her place of refuge—could be so horrible for him. While attempting to deeply understand another, she had to be open to her own associations. Although Melanie never discussed or processed with Grant her guess as to why fishing was important, the two of them were still able to become closer because of her empathic stance toward him, which helped Grant feel understood.

Validating Communicates Empathy

Emotional validation communicates to children that adults understand their perspective. Clinical experience suggests that validating can be used in a variety of settings, ranging from the consultation room to the classroom, and even to the athletic field. Emotional validation occurs in the following three ways: 1) through our behaviors; 2) by the words we choose; and 3) in the way we express our emotions, or our affect.

Validation Through Behavior

Adults can communicate that they understand or are trying to understand a young person's perspective through their behaviors. Mirroring, as a

Figure 3.1

therapeutic technique, provides non-verbal evidence that the adult understands the child. Just as looking into a mirror confirms or disconfirms our perception of ourselves, children require adults to act as mirrors, confirming their experiences, in order for them to organize their psychological landscapes. A classic childhood example of mirroring is when an infant gazes at his or her mother and the mother warmly looks back (Messer & Wolitzky, 1997). The classic example for adults is when a couple runs toward each other in an open field. Both lovers match the other's behaviors to show that they care.

To validate a child through mirroring, the therapist matches the child's behavior. The child frowns, the therapist frowns; the child nods in agreement and so does the therapist. In the classroom, this can be done through seating and body position. The teacher and pupil can sit side-by-side. The teacher can match the student's non-verbal communication. When the student shakes his head to indicate that he doesn't understand, the teacher follows suit. When providing tutoring, the teacher can make sure his or her eyes are level with the student's.

Validation Through Words

Children can be validated through language. This is distinct from providing good advice or counsel, which may paradoxically cause a child to retreat, explode, or shut down. The act of advising or questioning can remind a child who desires emotional connection that the adult questioning is in fact separate and not merged. The child may have been wishing that the adult could read his or her mind and when the grown-up seems not to do so, the child loses confidence in the communication. When children react poorly to good advice, sound interventions, or even reflective listening (listening to identify emotions such as "you sound angry"), it may mean that the child does not want the adult to ask questions, or even talk, because the child may wish that they share the same mind. Listening empathically can be very helpful, but sometimes children need even more from the relationship, a psychological closeness that transcends language. A grown-up can become emotionally closer by attempting to take the child's perspective.

Adults can demonstrate that they are striving to understand the child by choosing their words carefully. For example, when working with a child who is becoming upset, rather than saying, "You must feel awful," the adult could instead hypothesize with the child by asking, "How awful?" Rather than pointing out that the child is all alone in their own emotion, the second question demonstrates that the teacher is trying to understand how it might feel to go through whatever the child is experiencing. In this case, the adult is attempting to immerse himself or herself in the child's world. Psychologically, asking "how awful" is very different than defining an emotion or experience. By asking, the adult is providing language for the child's experience.

In clinical terms, this sort of approach in therapy is referred to as an "experience near" interpretation. It helps the client feel understood by the therapist (Kohut, 1959). But teachers, counselors, and any adult can use the same approach. The point is that the adult tries his or her best to take the child's perspective and empathically understand—not define—the emotion for him or her.

Child psychologist Skye Payne, PhD, recommends using the child's exact language, where possible, when attempting to validate a child through words. Of course, sometimes when adults use children's slang it can seem phony, prevents idealization, and can challenge generational boundaries. Generational boundaries are discussed later, but essentially they are the difference between children and adults. Children need adults to act like grown-ups who can serve as role models. Whenever possible and appropriate, with regard to generational boundaries, however, it is best to keep in mind the child's language when striving to communicate empathy.

Validation Through Affect

Affect validation is another, more sophisticated type of mirroring response (Stark, 2002). Affect is often confused with feeling. A feeling is something personal that occurs on the inside, while affect is the outside expression of the feeling. An example of affect validation is when a child proudly begins to master toilet training and his or her parents affirm the child's

  or

Figure 3.2

accomplishment. Both parents and the child feel proud and happy to be past the diaper stage and show it outwardly by their smiles and hugs. Another example is when a young person graduates from high school or college; the graduate feels validated when the happiness and sense of accomplishment he feels are shared by the adults that matter to him or her.

Interestingly, many theorists consider parental failure to affirm a child's toileting skills as an assault on the child's budding sense of self. To the child, the parents didn't understand the importance of his or her accomplishment. In this sense, the significance of toileting may be an opportunity for the infant's caregivers to succeed or fail in recognizing and validating the young child's significant developmental accomplishment.

Teachers and therapists are not generally working with children struggling with toilet training. But, if children are observed carefully, they will provide us with multiple opportunities to feel with them and demonstrate it through our affect in a way that helps children feel understood. In the therapy office, affect validation can take place when both therapist and client deeply and powerfully feel the loss of what might have been after a painful breakup. It can be the therapist sharing in the joy of an engagement or a

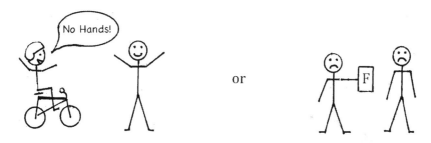

Figure 3.3

Figure 3.4

child's birth. In an educational setting, the teacher can celebrate the student's daily accomplishments, such as being able to count to 100 or to progress to the next reading level. The celebration can be over small successes or a big step like graduation. Because teachers spend so much time with students, they have countless opportunities to feel with them and demonstrate their empathy through their affect. The illustrations below demonstrate adults sharing feelings with children.

Empathy Case Study: Mad McCoy

Jamie McCoy, at 12 years old, hated and loved rules. She hated them because Jamie's family was in and out of incarceration because of rules. She loved them because rules, on the other hand, also kept her safe. Teachers couldn't break the rules by hurting her, taking her things, or otherwise abusing her. Despite her complex relationship with rules, and when angry Jamie saw "red," rules couldn't contain her. She had a history of angry violence toward peers and teachers. Jamie spent most of the school day running around the classroom or hiding from teachers. She was significantly behind in reading and on an Individual Education Plan for a reading disability.

The school system dreaded meeting with her parents. Jamie's mom and dad screamed profanity, called the teachers idiots, and threatened litigation or contacting the state's department of education and licensing boards. Although her parents never directly threatened physical violence, in meetings, they openly disclosed frightening prison stories with mature themes. Everyone's eyes widened. Teachers reported that they couldn't sleep the night before meetings. It became clear that the job of the meeting leader was to assess safety—not the typical emotional safety that occurs in special education meetings where difficult topics are discussed and parents have painful reactions, but to assess whether Jamie's parents were going to start a fist fight.

Jamie was in the fifth grade in a classroom with multiple adults. Her teachers' names were Jane and Helen. Jane liked Jamie and often spent her breaks playing games with her during recess. Helen wasn't consistently in the classroom, but helped out two days a week. One Monday morning she entered the room preparing to teach a lesson. Before beginning the lesson, Helen noticed a large cardboard box on the ground, picked it up, and threw it in the recycling bin.

From the corner of her eye, Jamie saw Helen throwing away the box. Jamie immediately began yelling obscenities then leapt from her chair and punched Helen hard in the chest. Helen fell backwards and another teacher had to physically restrain Jamie, who was furious. Helen was angry, confused, and hurt. What had happened?

After Jamie calmed, Helen learned that the empty cardboard box was very important to Jamie. When she was feeling overwhelmed, she would hide in the large box in the corner of the classroom. On this particular Monday, Jamie was emotionally upset about a distant relative who had reentered her life, and she was on edge from spending the weekend with him. The box was a way to feel sheltered from an interpersonally chaotic world where adults shouldn't be trusted. In Helen's attempt to tidy up the classroom, she inadvertently "took" Jamie's shelter.

After the incident, Helen attempted to take an empathic approach when processing with Jamie. "How terrible I took something important from you. I broke the rules," Helen said. Jamie quickly apologized and promised to never hit again. Next time, Jamie explained, maybe she could talk rather than hit.

Over the coming months, Jamie asked Helen if she could wear her scarf. Helen carefully taught Jamie how to tie the scarf around her shoulders. Jamie proudly wore it intermittently during the school day. One day, another child taunted Jamie for wearing an unlaundered shirt. "You wear the same dirty shirt every day, Jamie," she jeered. Jamie looked at the floor, shoving her hands deep in her pockets. Helen scowled and told the offending student that she, too, wore the same blue button-down shirt every day, so there! Jamie smiled. Helen smiled, too.

Eventually, Jamie asked if she could also wear Helen's favorite, stylish blazer. Jamie looked adorable with a long scarf to her knees, swimming in a large blazer. Jamie asked Helen, "How do I look?" Helen replied with, "You know Jamie, you and I are mostly the same." Although never directly spoken, it became clear to both of them that they had a special bond.

Later that school year, another student robbed Jamie of a special toy and then gloated about doing it. Jamie's face cinched down, her fists tightened, and she screamed a death threat in a murderous pitch. With tears in her eyes, Jamie walked herself to a cool-off area. She was furious. She and Helen sat together quietly. When Jamie calmed down, she told Helen how hurt and angry she was. Helen softly joked with Jamie to lighten up the situation by asking her if she was "kinda always mad?"

"Jamie why are you so mad?" Helen asked. Jamie laughed. "I'm a McCoy and McCoys are mad, that's why," she said.

Despite being clearly provoked and feeling rage, because of her relationship with Helen, Jamie was able to control her emotions better and refrained from punching the student who took her toy, something she probably would not have been able to do in the past.

Discussion

Before her relationship with Helen, Jamie's education had been a struggle. She had not allowed herself to connect with others and seemed to be on a downhill trajectory. Jamie, however, opened herself to allowing Helen to take an empathic stance. When Jamie wore Helen's clothes it wasn't just for fashion—it was an outward sign of the inward experience of seeing herself differently and of identifying with and idealizing Helen. Jamie, even at a young age, learned that she was not necessarily destined for misery. She could be anything or anyone she wanted, including a professional who wore scarves and blazers. Through her relationship with Helen—through feeling understood, accepted, and cared about—Jamie began to feel less vulnerable and reactive. She gained better control of her strong emotions. Ultimately, she felt safer in school and more confident about herself.

In summary, empathy is an important ingredient in the formation of meaningful relationships in the classroom. It is essential to understand the difference between sympathizing with a troubled student and empathizing with them, which means even if we can't give in to their anger and frustration, we can help them see that we understand why they are behaving in such a way. Doing so will help validate their internal and external experience and communicate that what they are feeling is real and appropriate for the situation. Validation through our behaviors, words, and affect are important ways to show empathy to children who need help developing a healthy sense of self. In the next chapter we explore belonging, the third ingredient in the Healing the Self model required to build strong relationships with children who struggle with poor self-esteem.

Learning Activities

Take a child's perspective by thinking of yourself as a teenager. Now imagine finally graduating from high school. You did it. You're closer to becoming a grown-up. What would you want your parents to feel? How might you want them to express their feelings? Next, imagine a first date that goes perfectly. Would you want your best friend to feel how important it was to you? How would you want that friend to express this?

Think of a time when you felt mirrored by an important adult. Write a paragraph or two about an instance in your childhood when important adults "got it." What was it like when you felt deeply understood by adults who cared for you? Perhaps they bought you the perfect gift, cooked your favorite dish, or said the perfect thing. Now write a paragraph describing your experience when someone important to you didn't understand your perspective. Did it anger you?

Application Activity

Write a paragraph or two about a specific time when you authentically shared in a child's triumph.

1. Did you feel proud of their accomplishment?
2. Did his or her success feel good to you?

Now, think of a time a child you work with became angry. Write a brief description of the incident. List at least three different things that you may have misunderstood. Everyone misses important aspects and, thank goodness, no one is perfect. The point of this exercise isn't to blame adults, but to simply begin the difficult process of exploring how empathy can reduce anger and violence.

References

Bacal, H. A. (1985). Optimal responsiveness and the therapeutic process. In A. Goldberg (Ed.), *Progress in self psychology* (pp. 202–227). New York, NY: The Guilford Press.

Kohut, H. (1959). Introspection, empathy, and psychoanalysis: An examination of the relationship between mode of observation and theory. In P. H. Ornstein (Ed.), *The search for the self* (Vol. 1, pp. 205–232). New York, NY: International Universities Press.

Messer, S. B., & Wolitzky, D. L. (1997). The traditional psychoanalytic approach to case formulation. In T. D. Ellis (Ed.), *Handbook of psychotherapy case formulation* (pp. 26–57). New York, NY: The Guilford Press.

Stark, M. (2002). *Working with resistance.* Northvale, NJ: Jason Aronson Publishers.

4 Belonging

We've all been in situations where we didn't feel like we belonged. At that moment, it's doubtful that we were at our best. That's because feeling like we belong is fundamental. We all need to feel like we fit in, we have a place, we matter, and we are part of something important. This is especially true for children. Children need to feel as if they belong to the adults in their world and to the groups of which they are a part. Children must feel they are wanted and are included in something bigger than themselves—a community that's there to protect and honor them, and to which they can contribute. A sense of belonging is so important that some thinkers believe that without it, children will not grow and adults will regress (Leary & Baumeister, 2017).

Belonging can be a life or death concern. Thomas Joiner, PhD, an international authority on suicide prevention, writes that a thwarted sense of belonging and sense of burdensomeness are the two most powerful predictors of suicide (Joiner, 2005). His empirically based, interpersonal model of identifying suicidal risk is considered a seminal psychological discovery. Of course, other variables need to be considered, but belonging is a crucial human need.

Because belonging is so important, it is the third relational ingredient in the Healing the Self model required to help children raise their self-esteem. Along with idealization and empathy, belonging is essential in enabling adults to create healthy relationships children can hold on to and heal through.

The belonging component of the Healing the Self approach is a more fluid and complex ingredient than idealization and empathy. Belonging is context-dependent. Someone may feel like they belong one moment, but not the next. When we have a sense of belonging, we can operate fully, so to speak, and be all that we are meant to be. When people feel they belong they can (Geist, 2008):

- Self-regulate
- Accomplish goals
- Know themselves
- Be self-aware
- Have close friends and stable relationships.

If people don't feel like they fit in and are unable to emotionally connect with others, they experience a reduction in their sense of self. Most humans strive to be around those they experience as like themselves, as was noted in Chapter 1. When they are not around these people they are not at their best (Ornstein, 1998). Put most simply, people need to be around other people who "get them" and who experience the world similarly. They need to be with people who communicate clearly that they are wanted and needed.

The remainder of this chapter is divided into two aspects of belonging: 1) feeling similar to someone, and 2) feeling emotionally close to them. It outlines in more detail how similarity and emotional closeness create a sense of belonging between two people when they think the same way and experience each other as deeply connected.

Feeling Similar

Most individuals naturally gravitate toward people who are more like them. Moreover, most people feel the best when they are surrounded by others they perceive to be somewhat like them. In this model of self-development, the presence of and connection to others are required for someone to be a healthy, independent individual (Lichtenberg, 1991).

In order to develop a sense of self, children must have access to someone they can experience as like them. As outlined in Chapters 2 and 3, to develop a child's self-esteem, this like-minded person must mirror the child and be someone the child can look up to or idealize, and thus connect with the child (Kohut, 1984). For example, imagine a boy imitating his father shaving. Not only is the boy idealizing the father as the father validates the child's mirroring play, but the boy also experiences a likeness to his dad. In other words, the boy silently understands that he and his father are similar and connected. This creates a sense of belonging in the child.

Fortunately, because being with like-minded people is a psychological need, children will often stretch themselves to be like-minded to the empathic adults to whom they have access. Conversely, there are loving, well-intentioned parents who just seem too different from their children. A slow tragedy unfolds when a child and parent struggle to feel similar to one another. It's heartbreaking when a child and parent can't stretch themselves to foster a sense of similarity. Sometimes children just don't seem to fit in with their families, and it is in precisely these instances when prepared and knowledgeable adults outside the family may make their greatest contributions.

Emotional Closeness

Feeling similar is important. But in order for children to develop a strong sense of self, they must also experience feeling deeply understood and accepted. This deep connection or emotional closeness is a construct that underlies both the empathy and idealization concepts of the Healing the

Self model. It is the simple idea that people need to be around and feel connected to like-minded others in order to feel whole (Geist, 2007).

Emotional closeness is typically thought to be experienced between an infant and their early caregivers. When an infant feels completely connected to his or her caregiver, it confirms this closeness. Some children, however, do not wish for closeness with others. This is thought to occur when, in the child's imagination, vulnerability is too risky. In such cases, the child retreats from them. In other words, the child thinks the adult cannot handle him or her, and so refrains from engaging (Lingiardi & McWilliams, 2017). As children mature, most expand their experience of closeness to include extended family members, teachers, and peers.

Of course, as long as there is genuine vulnerability, emotional closeness can occur with many different people and in different places. Clients might say "We have our own language," or "We both understand one another," when discussing their relationship with their therapist. An old psychotherapy joke involves the patient coming home from a session to his wife who asks, "How did it go?" The patient responds, "You wouldn't get it, it's between us." In the classroom, students might experience the same type of closeness with their teacher, especially if they are not emotionally close to their parents or caregivers at home. To such a child, class is special and the child feels that he or she is in tune with the teacher.

As children grow, most are able to generate a sense of closeness with their peers. This may occur on the athletic field, on a camping trip with a scout troop, or as a member of a faith-based organization.

A fictional, but outstanding, example of the development of emotional closeness in teens can be found in the 1985 film *The Breakfast Club*. Five very different students are able, through the adversity of suffering from an un-idealized and un-empathic principal, Mr. Vernon, to come together and experience a sense of similarity and closeness. The students realize, through interpersonally exploring their vulnerabilities, that they are more similar to each other than not and that they belong. In the film's conclusion, the independent students write an essay together and sign it as a group, "The Breakfast Club."

Such examples illustrate the importance of belonging and feeling a part of a group or relationship. As noted previously, feeling a sense of belonging is fundamental to our human nature—it is a basic human need. There is nothing more validating than being a part of a relationship or group in which you are made to feel important and cared for. For teachers and educators dealing with angry or violent children in their schools, this is the aim: to foster a connection with these children to help them feel as if they belong, even if only at school, so they can begin to heal and develop a stronger sense of self.

The preschool teacher, Melanie, who worked with Grant provides an excellent example of how this belonging can be fostered in the classroom. When Grant first came to the preschool, he felt unwanted and consequently acted out that rejection by punching and hitting. But by taking control of her class and agreeing to be the teacher and disciplinarian, Melanie communicated that at school, Grant belonged to her, the class, and his school. She made it clear to him that she wanted him there. She determined that sending him away when he misbehaved or allowing his angry outbursts in her classroom would not be helpful and would just reinforce his sense of abandonment. Instead, when Grant lashed out, she stayed close to him and he began staying near her. Congruently, when Grant's behavior calmed, his peers began to accept him more easily. Eventually Grant became part of the crew, which helped him develop a greater sense of self than any other "behavior modification" program the school could have instigated with him.

Belonging Case Study: Running the Bases

"No, get out of here. I can't do it," Aaron yelled at the top of his lungs. Tears of rage trickled down his cheek. Aaron was mad. Heidi, his classroom teacher, thought a game of kick ball would be fun for everyone, but Aaron's self-esteem was too low to enjoy it. He had successfully kicked the ball and made it to first base, but when he was asked to run to second base he melted down. On the surface, Aaron didn't think he could do it. Heidi wondered if his behavior really had more to do with frustrations at home than his athletic abilities.

Heidi reacted. "Aaron, when Bobby kicks the ball, run to the next base," she encouraged. Aaron, who had a history of violence, yelled louder. Other students responded to his yelling with both terror and excitement. Heidi, who had received training in the Healing the Self model, stepped back and took a breath. She knew this could explode. She felt herself becoming worried and wondered if Aaron felt worried, too.

Heidi imagined how demanding, intimidating, and scary the situation might be for Aaron. She knew that he had returned from a difficult visit with his mother and was likely on edge. As a college athlete herself she had always enjoyed sports. Thinking empathically and intuitively, she wondered if Aaron didn't feel good enough to run the bases alone. She tenderly said to him, "Aaron, let's do it together. I'll hold your hand."

She then reached out and held Aaron's hand in hers. Together, after Bobby punted the ball, Heidi and Aaron ran together, laughing as they sprinted to second base. Amazingly, the young teacher's assistant, Mr. Prewitt, who was also a former college athlete, missed the catch and fumbled the playground ball.

Seeing their chance to try for a homerun, Heidi cheered, "Let's do it!" Aaron, while holding Heidi's hand, ran the rest of the bases. Clumsily, Mr. Prewitt kept dropping the ball. Aaron and Heidi scored a homerun together, and Aaron beamed with pride. This triumph with Heidi was the beginning of feeling a sense of belonging for Aaron. He finally felt like a part of the team and that he had successfully contributed, with Heidi's help, to an outcome the whole group could be proud of.

After the game, Aaron and Heidi had a special connection. For the remainder of the year they appeared in tune most of the time. Aaron still had his ups and downs, but their connection was clear to everyone.

Discussion

Heidi took an empathic stance with Aaron. She tried to imagine what an insurmountable challenge running the bases could be for him. She imagined that Aaron was scared and didn't believe that he could do it. She quickly developed a hypothesis regarding the root of Aaron's outburst and developed a plan. By offering to run the bases together, she provided Aaron a sense of belonging. In this moment, Aaron belonged to her and she accepted him. The game was no longer a challenge that separated him from his classmates, and in this way he began to feel part of the class team as well. Kickball became an opportunity to become emotionally closer to a caring, empathic adult.

For the other kids running the bases was a snap, but not for Aaron. By offering to run the bases with him, not only did Heidi de-escalate the situation, but she also met his need to belong. Such an empathic response to Aaron also fostered his ability to look up to and idealize Heidi as the caring, compassionate professional she was.

In conclusion, belonging is a fundamental need. To be at their best, people need others around them whom they experience as emotionally close and similar. This sameness is an important childhood need required for the development of self-esteem. As children mature this need changes, but even adults require others who understand them in order to be at their best. In the next chapter we will explore more deeply how anger and aggression are the result of unmet empathic and belonging needs in children with low self-esteem, and how the Healing the Self model can be used to reduce rage and violence through applying its relational principles.

Learning Activities

Think of a time when you felt like you belonged to a peer group.

1. Did you feel similar or emotionally close to them?
2. What did this relationship to the group or a person in the group cause you to feel about yourself?
3. Was the experience empowering? Why or why not?

Write a short essay outlining when you felt like you belonged.

1. Can you think of why you felt connected to that particular group?
2. How would you describe the group of people, besides your family, that you most closely belong to?

Describe a time or an instance when you felt like an outsider to those around you.

1. What made you feel that way?
2. How might that situation have been remedied?
3. What was it like not to belong?

Application Activity

Make a list of at least three ways you could increase the sense of belonging with the children you work with. What activities, games, or lessons could assist in helping children feel a sense of togetherness? Share this list with a colleague. Can he or she provide helpful suggestions?

References

Geist, R. (2007). Who are you, who am I, and where are we going: Sustained empathic immersion in the opening phase of psychoanalytic treatment. *International Journal of Psychoanalytic Self Psychology, 2*(1), 1–16.

Geist, R. (2008). Connectedness, permeable boundaries, and the development of the self: Therapeutic implications. *International Journal of Psychoanalytic Self Psychology, 3,* 129–152.

Joiner, T. E. (2005). *Why people die by suicide.* Cambridge, MA: Harvard University Press.

Kohut, H. (1984). The self psychological approach to defense and resistance. In A. Goldberg (Ed.), *How does analysis cure* (pp. 13–33). Chicago: University of Chicago Press.

Leary, M. R., & Baumeister, R. F. (2017). *The need to belong: Desire for interpersonal attachments as a fundamental human motivation.* New York City: Routledge.

Lichtenberg, J. (1991). What is a self object? *Psychoanalytic Dialogues, 1,* 455–457.

Lingiardi, V., & McWilliams, N. (2017). *The psychodynamic diagnostic manual version 2 (PDM-2): Assessing patients for improved clinical practice and research.* New York, NY: The Guilford Press.

Ornstein, A. (1998). The fate of narcissistic rage in psychotherapy. *Psychoanalytic Inquiry, 18*(1), 55–70.

5 Understanding Anger and Aggression

The psychiatrist Anna Ornstein wrote that one way to understand mental illness and aggression is to simply view so-called disorders as ill-fated attempts to feel whole. Because idealization, empathy, and belonging are the necessary ingredients for developing a healthy self, a failure to experience these fundamental human needs results in psychological fragmentation and a breakdown of the self. Because a sense of self propels humans, they will take great measures to protect it (Ornstein, 1991). In this chapter, we explore how excessive anger and violence are the psychological costs when children do not sufficiently experience idealization, empathy, and belonging—the key ingredients in a healthy, restorative relationship.

Anger

Anger is part of the human experience. It is as important an emotion as joy, love, excitement, fear, and sadness. As children become adults, they learn how to feel, understand, and use all their emotions to inform decision-making. Children must be able to feel anger as well as all other emotions without unraveling. Doing so requires the right amount of frustration. Some children become too frustrated and can't seem to feel other uncomfortable feelings without turning them into anger, or worse, rage. The difference between anger and rage is subtle. An angry child can often see perspectives other than their own. An enraged child cannot see another's perspective.

Dr. Ornstein, an Auschwitz Nazi murder camp survivor, had firsthand experience with extreme acts of human anger and aggression. In her framework, anger, rage, aggression, and violence are not learned behaviors, but instead result from a low sense of self (Ornstein, 1991).

People often react to empathic failure—that is, when someone misses something important—with anger (Stark, 2002). Anger is complex and multi-determined, but when a child experiences empathic failure, in the child's mind, it can be a shattering assault and the child retaliates with feelings of anger. Anger provides a cohesive function, mimicking a sense of togetherness or an emotional bond. Anger is a temporary shortcut to having functional self-esteem.

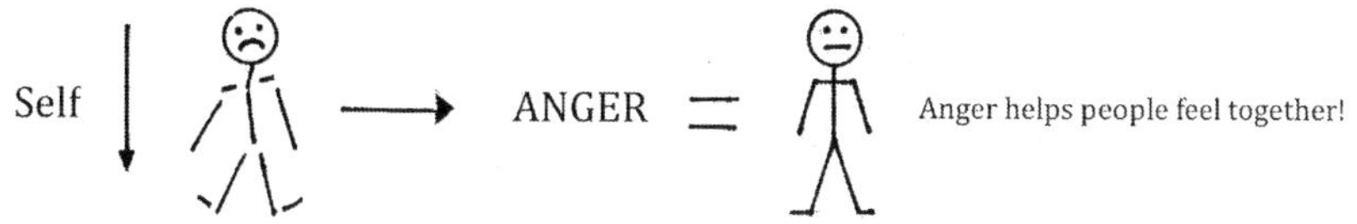

Self   ⟶   ANGER =   Anger helps people feel together!

Figure 5.1

If children become angry because they experience empathic failure, then perhaps empathic attunement can evaporate the fuel needed to drive their anger. This is not to say that teachers, therapists, or parents are entirely responsible for a child's feelings or that an adult could or should try to be perfectly empathic or in-tune with a child. However, empathic attunement does offer a way to better understand some of the dynamics of anger and some ways to reduce it in the consultation room, school, or home. Moreover, as children develop their self-esteem, their capacity to weather un-empathetic adults improves and their ability to develop their peer relationships increases.

Aggression

Over the years, psychology has had different assumptions regarding aggression. For our purpose here, aggression can be understood as a state that can serve to temporarily offer the aggressor a feeling of power. The aggressor feels powerful by demanding that others both superficially mirror and idealize him or her (Ornstein & Ornstein, 1993). Aggression can be verbal or physical, active or passive. It can be reactive or carefully planned. Regardless of the form of aggression, in some cases it can be diagnostic of a low sense of self. It may indicate that for the aggressor, these early developmental needs were unmet and they are now attempting to meet those needs the best way they can. Obviously, not every case of aggression is based on low self-esteem. People also have a stress model of flight, fight, or freeze. If you are hiking alone in the forest on the Appalachian Trail and are approached by an angry-looking bear, for example, your fear and perhaps anger are unlikely to be the result of feeling misunderstood by the bear. When children behave aggressively, they may be doing it so others idealize them and take their perspective.

Aggression as Idealization

When children are aggressive and violent, it's an attempt to force others to recognize their power. In this way, it's a form of idealization. For instance, when a child hits, it demonstrates his or her power and will to hurt others. In the child's mind, the one who hits is stronger (idealizable) than the weaker one, the victim who received the blow. Moreover, if the victim is injured, their pain reminds them of the attacker's (idealizable) power. Child may need others to idealize them because they haven't been able to idealize grown-ups. In this light, an aggressive child repeats the theme of idealization, the relational need that they lack. It's the child's backward attempt to meet their vital need of idealization. Interestingly, psychologist and philosopher Frank Summers writes that when countries require idealization from either their citizens or other countries, then there is an increased chance of international military conflict (Summers, 2016).

Aggression and Empathy

Ironically, empathy and violence are connected. This is because violence demands that others see things from the attacker's perspective. When a child is mad and hits, it forces the victim to know that the child is angry. In this light, violence is a bid for the victim to know the attacker's feeling state, and thus is similar to empathy. Violence demands that the victim "understands" something about the attacker. Imagine a child saying, "I hit you because I'm mad." The hit was an attempt for the adult to understand. Of course, violence never brings real closeness. The point, however, is to consider how violence can be understood as an attempt at empathy. Ironically, when children use aggression to be understood, the less others want to accept them—a vicious cycle may then ensue with more aggression and anger followed by more regression and withdrawal from peers, parents, and teachers.

Aggression can also be turned inwards. Children can hurt themselves. When children hurt themselves, it is because the physical pain may feel more manageable and predictable than the psychological pain of empathic disappointment. Moreover, children who self-harm do not possess the self-esteem necessary to regulate emotions. Self-harm, like other forms of violence, is an attempt to feel whole and in control.

A person generally has to go out of their way to be aggressive or violent. We call it being aggressive toward another person because it brings us to them, it doesn't move us away from them. Hence, violence or aggression is the opposite of indifference. It is intimate. Most healthy people do not behave aggressively toward strangers. Thus, contrary to common sense, a child's aggressive behavior may indicate a need for emotional closeness. Aggressive tendencies may dissipate when the need for closeness is met. For example, how many times have teachers moved a troubled child's desk

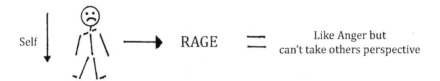

Figure 5.2

closer to theirs only to discover that it calmed the student? The proximity of the teacher may have helped the child feel closer and more connected, thus reducing their aggressiveness.

When a child uses a weapon as part of their aggression it may be an indication that he or she has lost the ability to take another person's perspective. In this light, aggravated assaults indicate that the child feels rage.

Defensiveness

Clinical wisdom suggests that people become defensive due to feelings of insecurity. That is, people are defensive out of fear that the other person won't understand them or be "like-minded." For psychotherapists, a client may become defensive out of fear that the therapist may poorly mirror them and not get them. In the case of children, they can become defensive in order to insulate themselves from feeling misunderstood by an adult (Shane, 1985). In the classroom, students may refuse to participate, act aggressively, or become disruptive as a preemptive defense against being misunderstood or harshly judged by their peers or teachers, who, in the angry child's mind, may not be able to handle their sense of inadequacy or brokenness.

Of course, when people feel terribly misunderstood by their therapist, caregivers, or teachers, it generally reveals that important others have previously misunderstood them. The illustration below demonstrates the disappointment and anger of feeling misunderstood by an important other.

Feeling misunderstood followed by acting aggressively becomes a cycle. In therapy, a therapist may invite patients to replicate and work through this experience so they can heal from it and move on in their lives. Therapy requires fully feeling powerful feelings, often unpleasant ones, toward the therapist, whom the patient learns to forgive. When this happens, the patient can forgive themselves and ultimately move on. In the classroom, teachers can of course recognize when they misunderstand a student. Often, a brief acknowledgement can go a long way to helping a dysregulated student return to the difficult task of learning. Next, we examine how the relational ingredients of idealization, empathy, and belonging increase anger and violence when they are unmet.

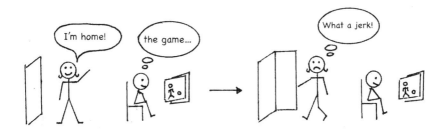

Figure 5.3

Figure 5.4

Unmet Idealization

When children haven't been able to idealize special adults, they can demand that other people then idealize them. These children tend to act out feelings. They can be precocious and distrustful. Their relationships tend to be inauthentic and phony. They can be show-offs, embellish stories, need fancy things to feel important, find a kind of shallow self-worth in the exclusive company of attractive or accomplished people, or suffer from substance abuse. If the child's parent is addicted, instead of seeing substance abuse as the parent's problem, children may see this as damaging their idealized version of their parent and ultimately damaging their own ability to build lasting, real self-esteem.

Unmet Empathic Needs

When empathic needs are not fully met in early childhood relationships, children may attempt to meet them in later relationships, often in a variety of unhealthy ways. Such children may have difficulty developing their own perspective or identity (Sherwood & Cohen, 1994). Conversely, they may become upset when others don't take their perspective. When children can't form their own perspective they become social chameleons. They rarely rock the boat and tend to be very agreeable. They seldom believe they have a problem and are difficult to help as adults.

One outcome of not having empathic needs met is trouble being empathic toward others. When children demand that others endlessly take their perspective, it can be maddening for everyone. People who engage in the world this way often harbor deep feelings of inadequacy. They can be very sensitive and need others to validate their experiences and reality. Heinz Kohut believed that needing validation and needing others to see things our way is a normal stage of development, but that some people remain stuck in it (Kohut, 1972). Of course, healthy people also require empathy, but they can generally tolerate another person's perspective.

Figure 5.5

Unmet Belonging

When children do not have a sense of belonging, they will often try to find a group to which they can feel like they belong. They may over-identify with a subculture or group, such as an anti-social gang. Of course, the pseudo-belonging that gangs and other bad groups provide can be very dangerous.

Sometimes young people seek out belonging through intense, immature romantic relationships. Unfortunately, some teens may define themselves through their relationships—an external identity rather than a genuine expression of their inner selves. However, these relationships will only provide them with a false sense of wholeness, which will do more to inhibit than to promote growth. Unmet belonging can often be seen in romantic relationships in which teenagers don't have the self-esteem to function as independent people. Such relationships may be based solely upon simply agreeing with one another. In this sense, the relationship is far from mature.

A sense of belonging is such an important need that children will also sometimes modify their language to meet it. This is why they may use offensive language or slang. Sadly, this subculture approach may actually distance the child from important others and can be a way of hiding the vulnerability needed for real belonging.

Anger and Aggression Case Study: Angry Andre

"Fuck, fuck, fuck," Andre chanted as he circled the room. His teacher pleaded, "Andre, please stop saying that." Andre replied, "Fuck you!" He then threw two chairs at her and ran out of the room.

Andre was a nine-year-old third grader. He was a little guy with a big personality who strutted around the classroom like the boss. Most of the time the look on his face said, "Stay the hell away from me!" Other times, he would be sweet and seek out closeness with his teachers. Despite being very smart and academically above grade-level, Andre rarely attended his regular classroom; it overwhelmed him. He also avoided doing simple school work. At the end of first grade he was placed in a smaller classroom for children with emotional and behavioral problems due to his disruptive aggressiveness. Andre had a history of violent behavior, mostly directed at adults like his mother or teachers. In second grade, he attacked a teacher and seriously injured her leg. His mother called the police twice because Andre threatened to stab her with a kitchen knife. Occasionally, he went after a classmate, but this was rare.

Dan, a counselor in the school, invited Andre to meet with him. Dan was new to the school and new to Andre. Before they met, Dan recalled asking a colleague about the "angry little boy." The colleague replied, "He's a lot of anger in a small package."

During early meetings with Dan, Andre was flip and sarcastic toward him. Having been trained in the Healing the Self model, Dan decided to spend more time just listening to see what he could learn. Andre would go on rants about his "piece of crap" mother and "butt hole" father. He directed his anger at his parents for forbidding video game time or not buying him a cell phone. He would also rage about school work, saying it was easy "baby stuff."

Dan hypothesized that Andre felt disconnected from his parents and took comfort and distraction in video games. Both his parents had their own struggles, and his father lived far away. Andre was often put in foster care and placed with a different caregiver, which he both embraced and resented. Andre couldn't easily admire his parents because of legal and substance abuse issues. Dan suspected that at the heart of Andre's school-work refusal was a sense of alienation, worry, and perfectionism. Andre's anger and frustration masked his worry and managed his relationships. As much as he wanted closeness with others, it scared him; he didn't know what to do with it.

In their next meeting, Dan observed that Andre's worries consumed him. Dan sat quietly and listened. It became clear that Andre looked up to Dan and valued their meetings. Dan was calm, thoughtful, and real with him. Andre knew exactly what to expect from Dan. Meanwhile, Dan did his best to deeply understand Andre, who began to feel connected with Dan—maybe Andre felt heard and understood by Dan. The two of them became close.

One day, Andre confided to Dan that he really didn't want to be so angry any longer and didn't "like" breaking the rules and hoped to return to a typical classroom. The two of them developed a plan. "The Plan" was that whenever Andre became angry or frustrated, Dan or his teacher would remind him of his goal by saying, "Remember our plan."

Shortly after that meeting, Dan walked into the classroom and saw Andre frustrated and escalating with another student. This might become violent,

Dan thought to himself. Dan walked up to Andre and said, "Andre, remember our plan." Andre stopped and looked at Dan over his shoulder. Although still furious, Andre just stood there for a moment. Dan said, "Do you want to come visit with me for a minute?" Andre nodded and followed him. The bond between Andre and Dan had helped Andre avoid a possible fist fight and peacefully calm down.

Discussion

Andre worried and doubted his own ability to control his emotions, was angry, and behaved violently. Before Dan made the effort to connect with him, Andre regularly lost self-control and attacked adults and children. By developing a strong relationship with Dan, Andre was able to settle down. Andre looked up to Dan, Dan was empathic, and together they developed a sense of belonging. Andre realized that Dan wasn't afraid of his anger and wouldn't banish him for being mad. Dan strove to imagine what it was like for Andre and hypothesized what feelings lay beneath his rage.

When Dan and Andre forged "Their Plan," it served not only as a course of action but as a ritual and special code between them. The phrase "Remember our plan," reminded Andre of his connection with Dan. This togetherness enabled Andre to step back and reconsider his actions. Andre felt cared for, understood, and liked by Dan. Dan liked Andre, too, and in a sense, they belonged to each other. Maybe this belonging was as new to Andre as his new ability to control himself. Dan's deep, close connection with Andre didn't remove all of Andre's worries or life's troubles, but it enabled him to feel proud of himself and his newfound ability to self-regulate his emotions and behaviors.

In summary, the Healing the Self model considers aggression as an attempt to feel whole. Aggression temporarily provides a feeling of togetherness that mimics durable self-esteem. Childhood anger grows from empathic failure. What helps children suffering from too much anger is a deep understanding. What cures them is the development of lasting self-esteem.

Learning Activity

Write a paragraph describing when you have felt angry with someone close to you.

1. What was misunderstood on both sides?
2. Was there a relational component?
3. How would empathy have changed the situation?
4. Do you imagine that you may have felt less angry if the other person had understood your perspective?
5. Were you able to talk about it later?
6. Did doing so bring you and the other person closer?

Application Activity

Think of aggression as an attempt to feel whole. Think of ways you could help the children you work with avoid having to be aggressive. Of course, it is impossible to prevent all aggression and anger, but list things you could do to increase how the children you work with could more readily idealize you. How could you strive to be more empathic while increasing the sense of belonging? Although easy to write, this action may be difficult to do. Be mindful that no one can perfectly be idealizable, empathic, or have a flawless sense of belonging with the children they work with.

References

Kohut, H. (1972). Thoughts on narcissism and narcissistic rage. In P. Ornstein (Ed.), *The search for the self: Selected writing of Heinz Kohut*, 1950–1978. New York, NY: International Universities Press.

Ornstein, A. (1991). When the patient is demanding. In H. Jackson (Ed.), *Using self psychology in psychotherapy* (pp. 155–166). Northvale, NJ: Jason Aronson Publishers.

Ornstein, P., & Ornstein, A. (1993). Assertiveness, anger, rage, and destructive aggression: A perspective from the treatment process. In R. A. Glick & S. P. Roose (Eds.), *Rage, Power, and Aggression* (pp. 102–117). New Haven, CT: Yale University Press.

Shane, M. (1985). Summary of Kohut's "The self psychological approach to defense and resistance." In A. Goldberg (Ed.), *Progress in self psychology* (Vol. 1, pp. 69–79). New York, NY: The Guilford Press.

Sherwood, V., & Cohen, C. (1994). *Psychotherapy of the quiet borderline patient; The As-if personality revisited.* New York, NY: Jason Aronson, Inc.

Stark, M. (2002). *Working with resistance.* Northvale, NJ: Jason Aronson Publishers.

Summers, F. (2016). The United States of America and the glorification of violence. *Psychoanalytic Inquiry, 36*(6), 488–496. doi:10.1080/07351690.2016.1192392

6 When in Crisis . . .

As outlined previously, childhood anger and aggression are often the result of empathic failures. That is, important people who are supposed to understand something important, don't. Whereas the previous chapter explained the foundation for understanding anger and aggression, this chapter focuses on providing parents, teachers, therapists, and childcare workers with a systematic approach that has been demonstrated to assist young people in de-escalating an emotional crisis. Of course, what truly de-escalates a child is a relationship with an adult, but this chapter provides concepts that may be useful when confronted by a crisis.

De-escalation is not a natural talent, but a set of skills that can be learned, practiced, and refined. The following outlines de-escalation strategies. The premise of this chapter is that adult self-awareness is the primary factor in de-escalating a child. The secondary factors for crisis de-escalation are adult debriefing, teamwork, and parallel process.

What Is a Crisis?

By increasing someone's self-esteem you increase their ability to control their emotions and thereby reduce crisis. This occurs because the healthy aspects of a positive relationship with an adult become absorbed into the child's personality. Healing the Self is the application of a relationship with a trusted adult who is empathic toward the child. Because the child looks up to this trusted adult, the child feels connected. Conversely, negative adult relationships or peer relationships can also become absorbed into the child's mind and serve as a negative influence (Miller, 1996).

There are different types of crisis and violence. A crisis or violent outburst can be the result of a brain injury, seizure, or other neurological event. Sometimes what appears to be an emotional crisis can be a calculated attempt to push limits, engage in a preferred activity, and/or air resentment. However, most crises, for most children, are reactive in nature; they are an expression of emotional turmoil and are not premeditated (Family Life Development Center, 2001). The ideas in this chapter are useful for adults to consider when addressing reactive-type aggression. Of course, this process is not meant to replace a psychological, psychiatric, or neurological exam.

What Should Be Done?

For a reactive-type crisis, there are four steps to be taken in the heat of the moment. Of course, the best time to prevent a crisis is by proactively building a relationship between an adult and a child where the child admires the adult, the adult empathizes with the child, and together there is a sense of belonging. But in the cases where crisis occurs, the following are specific steps that de-escalate angry, out-of-control children.

Step One: Stop!

Beginning with Sigmund Freud, psychology has a long-established tradition of using military metaphors. This may be because of the war-torn era in which Freud lived. Keeping with that tradition, military examples can be used when discussing crisis. US Navy Commander Mark Devine suggests that when in crisis, first, stop (Devine, 2013). The adult should start by not doing anything. Similarly, Dr. Theodore Ellenhorn suggests that when the therapist feels it is necessary to act, it's often because the therapist has allowed themselves to become wrapped up in the patient's internal world. When you feel you have to act, that's because you have lost perspective. While any adult who works with small children knows that there are times when quick thinking and acting is necessary, this model states that in a crisis, the adult should first stop. Clinical wisdom suggests that a moment to pause actually increases the overall efficiency required when tasked with making a good decision.

Step Two: What I Am Doing?

The second step in crisis intervention is self-awareness. Self-awareness is the primary intervention for crisis de-escalation (Family Life Development Center, 2001). This is because empathy requires self-awareness. Empathy necessitates knowing and then bracketing your own experience to think, feel, sense, and imagine another person's experience (please review Chapter 4 for more information regarding empathy). But what is self-awareness? Self-awareness is the process of asking yourself, "What am I—?"

- Doing
- Thinking
- Feeling
- Sensing
- Hoping

"What am I doing? How am I using my body? Am I sitting, standing, pacing? Am I still or moving? If so, at what speed?" The first step to self-awareness is recognizing one's behaviors.

"What is my body communicating to me regarding my emotional and physical experience at this moment regarding the situation?" We must be able to feel and manage our own feelings while still being rational in order to use them constructively.

"What am I thinking? Am I thinking, 'I should be able to control this situation?' Am I thinking of something else entirely? Am I trying to distract myself with my thoughts? Am I trying to 'figure it out' so I don't have to feel a nasty feeling?"

"What am I feeling? Do I feel bored, angry, ashamed, excited? Does this feeling state remind me of something awful in my own history? Does this feeling state pleasantly distract me from something else?"

"What am I sensing?" Not that your sense or intuition is accurate or provides you with "facts" about the other person, but it does provide you with "facts" regarding your *experience* with the other person. In short, your experience of the situation provides you with incredibly important information regarding your understanding of the situation.

"What am I hoping?" Hope is significant because many contemporary psychological theories suggest that hope and wishes drive human experience. What people wish for fuels their most intimate inner experiences. An old barber's joke explains this concept well: "I'm not angry because I'm balding, I'm angry because I hoped to always stay young."

Knowing your experience with an escalated child is necessary for two reasons. First, ask yourself if you are unintentionally escalating the child. That is, are you helping the situation or hurting? Second, empathizing with the child demands knowing your own experience. This is because empathy requires the ability to distance yourself from your own experience in order to imagine someone else's. This practice is known as bracketing. Bracketing involves consciously taking your experience, naming it, and understanding it to prevent it from polluting your ability to understand something outside yourself more deeply (Small, 2001).

Bracketing is associated the philosopher Edmund Husserl, who wrote about understanding the human experience. Not only does the process of bracketing assist in preventing someone's preconceptions from interfering, but the process of bracketing may actually increase the adult's ability to delve deeper into his or her understanding of themselves in relation to a subject (Tufford & Newman, 2010). This being said, some theorists wonder if it's ever truly possible to completely know your own preconceptions, let alone prevent them from influencing your ability to know something (Creswell, 1994).

Step Three: What Is the Relational Need the Child Is Communicating?

Current thinking in psychology suggests that whenever, for whatever reason, a child isn't protected from emotions that are too strong for him or her to understand, they grow up to develop defensive methods for "feeling" difficult emotions (Stolorow, 1999). Stolorow believes that these maladaptive ways, however they may manifest, have two key features: avoiding emotions that are too powerful for them to handle and seeking connection with an adult who hopefully can handle the powerful feeling (Stolorow, 2007). First, the child's difficulties are an effort to mitigate a sense of fragmentation that may accompany powerful feelings. In a way, a child's misbehavior is an attempt to escape negative, disorganizing feelings. Second, the crisis is the child's best attempt for the adult to understand something important. The third step in de-escalation, therefore, is to ask yourself what the child needs. That is, what is his behavior asking for? In this way the parent, teacher, or counselor develops a guess or hypotheses regarding the child's needs (Colvin & Sugai, 1989). A hypothesis is an idea that can then be tested.

Step Four: Understand

Once the adults have developed a hypothesis, they need to test it. In other words, if the behavior is an attempt to meet a real or imagined need, how could adults meet that need? In this light, adults are seeking to understand the child as well as protect him or her from feelings that are too strong for the child to bear alone. Examples of meeting children's needs may include providing:

- A quiet place
- Warmth
- A good listener
- A distraction

Arguably, the need itself may not be important at all. The crisis may in fact be an effort, outside of the child's awareness, for the adult to do something different in his or her attempt to meet the child's need. What may assist the child in better dealing with his or her emotions is that a caring adult attempted to meet that need. Meeting children's needs means that the adult understood the child and together they were able to develop a bond. In short, de-escalation is empathy in action.

Why This Works

Knowing your experience is vital to effectively de-escalate a crisis for four interrelated reasons. It is required for bracketing your experience, so you can better develop an empathic hypothesis regarding the child's. It's also necessary so that adults can:

- Know their limits.
- Understand the child's feelings.

- Contain the child's feelings.
- Change the outcome.

Know Your Limits

It is natural and expected for invested adults working with children to periodically feel provoked, annoyed, or worse, by a child's provocative behaviors. The adults must first be aware of their emotions in order to prevent these feelings from influencing their judgment and actions (McKay, Fanning, Paleg, & Landid, 1996). Parenting a troubled child is exhausting, while working with challenging children rewards and taxes us simultaneously. Adults must recognize when they have become too emotionally charged to effectively de-escalate children egregiously acting out. Moreover, young people, for many reasons, may purposefully try to "trigger" us; it is important that adults know themselves enough to recognize when they have reached their limits.

When adults try to fool themselves into believing that they don't have ill feelings toward a child or a difficult situation, it leads to divestment in the child and "burn-out." In my experience, many children counter their caregiver's reduction in investment by increasing their acting out. Crisis demands attention. If a child doesn't feel attended to, he or she may generate a crisis to meet this need. Simply put, pretending you're not upset is actually quite likely to lead to an escalation of misbehavior.

Anger is okay. It is a natural emotion, and for adults the first step is recognizing when you are feeling angry, and then accurately assessing how anger, boredom, frustration, irritation, or any other feeling is affecting your judgment. Donald Winnicott, a pediatrician and psychotherapist, famously wrote that many of his therapy patients didn't get better until he recognized that he "hated" their troublesome behaviors and how they affected him (Winnicott, 1949). Moreover, he wrote that it was necessary for the therapist to both be aware of his or her feelings and emotionally survive the interaction. Of course, it can be damaging to ever tell a child that you dislike him or her. Think of the classic teacher saying, "I like you, but I don't like your behavior." The key idea is that your internal world offers important clues regarding another person's experience.

Anger is part of the human experience. Humans must be able to feel anger, as well as all emotions, without unraveling, and this requires noticing, understanding, and using frustration. Nevertheless, some people become too angry or can't seem to feel other uncomfortable feelings without turning them into anger, or worse, rage.

Assessing your own negative feelings, especially anger, however, can be very difficult! Research from Cornell University indicates that anger compromises everyone's thinking ability: "When we are at our angriest, we are at our stupidest" (Family Life Development Center, 2001, p. 49). Self-awareness offers a vital check regarding when adults have surpassed their limit and another adult must step in to provide care for a child. Moreover, if a care provider finds themselves consistently overwhelmed, it is vital that they seek support. Understanding if you are past your limit requires both introspection and extrospection.

Introspection is necessary, but alone it is insufficient to assess if you have surpassed your bandwidth. Introspection is asking yourself what clues you noticed when you lost your cool. It is listening carefully to yourself and observing your inner and outer states. Did you:

- Feel warm
- Experience sweat
- Tap your foot
- Have an increased heartrate
- Cry
- Lock yourself in the bathroom
- Zone out
- Eat
- Drink alcohol
- Use nicotine
- See red

Dr. Raymond Chin, a neuropsychologist and mindfulness and Tai Chi expert, describes mindfulness practices as a wonderful way to increase anyone's ability to self-observe. By mindfulness, Dr. Chin means the cultivation of awareness by focusing attention on the present moment, purposefully and without judgment. Mindfulness hones attention to the present moment, away from past regrets and future doubts. In his practice, he finds that mindfulness increases awareness of oneself and others, calms the autonomic nervous system and impulses, and promotes the neutrality necessary for decision-making. It has been demonstrated to assist with symptom reduction if practiced regularly by those with ADHD, mood disorders, pain due to illness, trauma, etc. Mindfulness cannot be taught by someone who does not practice it because to understand it you must experience it. Of course, everyone can benefit from practicing mindfulness. Mindfulness has been repeatedly demonstrated to aid in decision-making and can serve as a psychological treatment modality (Kabat-Zinn & Williams, 2013).

Introspection, however, has its limitations. Extrospection, or seeking outside help in assessing your level of frustration, is also vital. After the incident, when you and your student are calm, ask a trusted colleague what he or she noticed about you. Seeking outside perspectives regarding our own behaviors is necessary for us to grow in our ability to handle both our own emotional worlds and those of our students. People have a limited capacity to self-observe—this is why elite athletes have coaches—and why it's standard practice to receive a second opinion before surgery.

Of course, the best way to understand your own emotions and increase your capacity to understand others is to engage in your own psychotherapy.

Some treatment models of talk therapy are emphatic that patient change is impossible without the therapist honestly undergoing his or her own therapy. This is because personal therapy is required for the therapist to determine whose emotions are whose.

The following psychotherapy example of a therapist past his limit clarifies the concepts of introspection and extrospection. A patient was disclosing to his therapist his idea to murder his pregnant girlfriend. It was important to note that the patient didn't have a plan, but wondered aloud how freeing it would be to kill someone who was pregnant. The therapist, whose own wife was expecting, dissociated or completely zoned out and began daydreaming about a particular café in France. This worried the therapist; how could he listen and help this person if he kept thinking of coffee in little, white, porcelain cups? He was clearly past his limit. When the patient spoke, the therapist immediately "went" to the Alps.

Through introspection, the therapist understood that he was dissociating and leaving his patient stateside. He knew he was completely checked out, and the treatment was at a standstill. It wasn't until he used extrospection (supervision from a trusted mentor) that he came to understand his own emotional bandwidth, and that he "went" to France because it was too much for him. He didn't understand what was happening between himself and his client. Ultimately, he learned his response to his patient provided him with critical information. First, the therapist learned that understanding people and concepts made life less traumatizing for him! If he could understand something, then it wasn't so bad for him. Second, he became aware of a series of vital questions that enabled the patient to grow in the therapy: did the patient want others to flee from him? Did he want people who cared about him to abandon him? When these hypotheses and others were explored in therapy, the patient no longer needed to scare his therapist.

After the therapist explored these questions, the patient stopped obsessing about murder. The therapist learned, too, by understanding what the patient was saying symbolically, and the client was freed to discuss other things. The therapist got it, and the client improved. As the treatment progressed, the therapist learned that the patient's girlfriend wasn't even pregnant; the patient created the story, and others like it, just to push people away from him.

Understand

It is necessary to try to understand your own feelings in order to understand others. This is because emotions are contagious (Bowen, 1974; Goldenberg & Goldneberg, 2004). Until a child has developed his or her sense of self or self-esteem, he or she requires others to feel either *with* or *for* them, or a combination of the two. Has your heart ever gone out to a child? Have you really felt happy, sorry, or sad for him or her? In these instances, you are feeling *with* the child. You two are sharing the same emotional experience. Clinical wisdom suggests that when adults feel with children it provides children an intimate model for how to experience feelings.

Children also require adults to feel *for* them. Have you ever worked with a student who seemed to purposely provoke you? It seemed that they felt glad for your misery! Children without a solid psychological core don't have the capacity to feel all the emotions that emerge within them. Therefore, rather than feeling these often unpleasant emotions, they behave in ways that give that emotion to another person. These children play "hot potato" with nasty feelings in an effort to avoid feeling them. When a child gives the adult his or her feeling, he or she is also hoping that the adult will demonstrate how to experience the emotion, thereby reducing the emotion's intensity and enabling the child to feel it more safely. In this light, troublesome behavior is both a way to avoid negative emotions and an attempt at connecting to another.

Because growing children require adults to feel with and for them, understanding ourselves is critical. Our own feelings provide important clues to understanding the child's emotional experience. When care providers strive to use their own emotionally colored perceptions, reactions, and thoughts to better understand children, it offers insights into the child's experience.

For instance, say a student is escalating. The adult feels powerless. The adult's sense of powerlessness may be a feeling that he or she is experiencing *with* or *for* the child. Her sense that she can't do anything may indicate that:

- The child feels powerless. (Feeling with the student)
- The child felt powerless, but now feels happy because he or she has proved his or her power by making someone else feel powerless. (Feeling for the student)

Moreover, children need adults to feel their feelings with them and to be emotionally close to them. In infancy, when an infant cries, the mother or father picks up the child and they share an emotional connection. Children develop their capacity to feel, use, and understand their emotions through their relationships with important adults.

When adults strive to understand their feelings, thoughts, and wishes regarding a child, that awareness lays the foundation for a healthy feeling-sharing process to occur. Conversely, if adults run on an unconscious "auto pilot," lasting growth is blocked. Emotional growth requires realness from everyone.

Contain

When adults recognize their own negative emotions, and maturely handle them, it communicates to children that people can feel a wide range of emotions without having to act on them. It demonstrates to children many things about their emotional worlds, including that emotions:

- Are not scary.
- Are natural.
- Can be understood.
- Can be informative.
- Do not need to be acted out.

When adults allow themselves to feel the emotions that bubble up inside them during a crisis, it provides the child with a sense of relief. This is because it communicates that emotions can be felt and contained. That is, horrible feelings can't really harm you. People can experience emotions without being ruled by them. Feelings inform us, but don't have to run the show. Not only can powerful feelings enrich our lives, powerful feeling can bring us together. People connect with others by sharing strong emotions (Nicholson, Perez, & Kurtz, 2019). Similarly, when adults disavow their own emotional experience, it communicates to children that emotions are beyond understanding or worse, are to be feared. Some therapists, such as Jessica Benjamin, believe that when the adult can't recognize their own feelings it prevents them from really "recognizing" the other. That when therapists don't know themselves, it makes it very difficult for the patient to grow or have his or her own identity (Benjamin, 2010).

Change Outcome

Finally, adults must assess their emotional experience with children in order to change the emotional context of the crisis. The following highlights the emotional context of a crisis. For example:

A. Jon provokes Bob. Bob becomes angry. Bob hits Jon. The emotional context for Bob is anger and frustration.
B. Jon provokes Bob. Bob becomes angry. Bob's teacher Joan intervenes. Bob calms. The emotional context is a feeling of security and comfort with Joan.

Clinical wisdom suggests that children in crisis often repeat the same difficulties. Their explosions can become a predictable madness. Again, it's a child's attempt to both insulate themselves from too-powerful emotions and seek connections. Adults working with these children often find themselves doing the same failed interventions again and again. It is as if everyone is following a secret script that ends with the same tragic, unhappy result. When adults examine their own feelings, thoughts, and wishes, it provides them an escape from mindlessly "playing a role in someone else's internal drama" and changes the emotional context of the crisis (Boyer & Giovacchini, 1993,

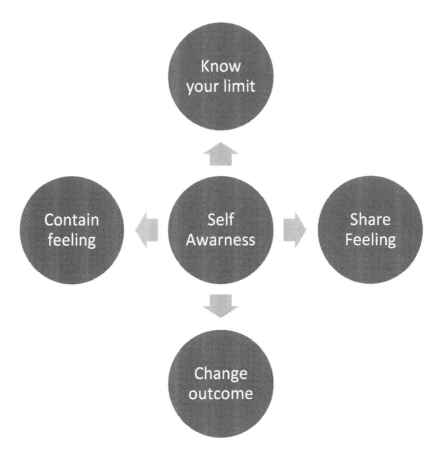

Figure 6.1

p. 79). When the adult understands his or her feelings regarding the child and the situation, the emotional context between the young person and the adult is fundamentally changed (Mehrabian, 1981). This is critical because changing the context of the relationship is necessary in order to change the meaning of the emotions and to foster psychological growth.

Additional Factors in De-Escalation

Adult debriefing, teamwork, and parallel process are the secondary interventions used in crisis de-escalation. They are secondary because working with others and disclosing aspects of the patient-provider experience enables the adult to become emotionally closer with his or her team and facilitates greater self-awareness. The following outlines how debriefing and teamwork lead to increased self- awareness.

Adult Debriefing

Working with challenging children can be exhausting. We may love what we do, but everyone has his or her limits. One way to reduce fatigue following a difficult day is for the adults to debrief and process the event(s) with other adults working in the school. Clinical wisdom suggests that when adults have a time and place to openly discuss an event and process it, they can change the emotional context of the difficult day for themselves; this allows them to both let go of the event and to grow from it. Without this time to process, people are likely to take the difficult day home, or worse, take it out on someone else. Interestingly, one of the first therapists to write about people taking frustration out on innocent others who were not involved in the incident was a young women named Anna Freud—Sigmund Freud's daughter! Experience suggests that if adults are not given the opportunity to process difficult days in a productive manner they will:

- Feel burned out
- Disinvest in students
- Feel hopeless themselves
- Increase substance use ("I need a glass of wine after today!")

Debra Lopez, MD, professor of psychiatry at the Robert Larner College of Medicine at the University of Vermont, suggests using what you were imagining to connect to your peer. When you are caught in a certain place with a student and you can't think through how to become unstuck, discussing it with other staff members may open things up between the student and the teacher, and give the teacher a chance to return to the student without feeling like a failure. Can you use your personal experience to better connect with trusted peers? Being aware of these aspects of your experience (introspection), and disclosing them to trusted peers and seeking their insights (extrospection), can lead to emotional growth for the student.

However, if the process of the tough day becomes routine, then every day is discussed the same way with little change, as if the process itself is simply another scene in the recurring drama. This may indicate that the student and teacher need additional help. Some authors suggest that true emotional growth only occurs after the therapist and the client find themselves "stuck," enacting the same drama over and over again. Harvard psychiatrist Paul Russell termed this dilemma the "Crunch." He writes that the patient and the therapist have to go through it and survive it in order to grow. People can't grow past their own suffering until another joins them in it, Russell explained. Closeness to others is what allows people to grow (Russell, 2006).

Teamwork

Without teamwork, individual self-awareness will only work inconsistently and cannot provide lasting growth. Everyone involved in crisis de-escalation must continually strive to be on the same page and share the ethic of self-examination. It is to be expected that "difficult to teach" children will act as if one adult is all "good" and another is all "bad." This is a common way that children attempt to thwart the adults' good intentions and test the adults around them. If all the adults work together, however, it greatly reduces the likelihood and severity of adults being pitted against one another. This requires that the adults agree to provide a unified front and cultivate an ethic of professional trust among them. Teamwork and cooperation among the adults is crucial.

Parallel Process

The notion of parallel process is another important but indirect component of de-escalation. The concept of parallel process has changed over the years, and was first written about by Dr. Harold Searles. Originally, it was defined as the phenomenon in which difficulties between psychotherapy patients and their therapists seemed to bleed into the therapist/supervisor relationships (Searles, 1955). That is, in some cases, the patient's difficulties become mirrored between the therapist and the therapist's supervisor. Parallel process was considered similar to the opening of Pandora's Box. The emotional difficulties of the child flowed to the adult working with the child, then to the adult's supervisor. In the 1980s, parallel process increasingly became considered bidirectional, meaning that not only does the patient's struggles influence the relationship between the therapist and their supervisor, but that struggles between the therapist and their supervisor filtered down and impacted the patient. Parallel process was then expanded to include cultural issues, meaning that the cultural identity of therapists also filters down through the patient, therapist–supervisor dyad. Moreover, the notion of parallel process can be overused, too, and be a way of blaming our own difficulties on the very people we are there to assist (Watkins, 2012). Despite being written about, few empirical studies measure parallel process and therefore not all psychologists ascribe to it (Watkins, 2017).

Current education models expand parallel process to understand the conflicts between teachers and administrators when teachers work with traumatized children (Nicholson et al., 2019). They write that, in the simplest sense, how principals and other administrators treat their faculty will mirror how the faculty treat their students. Teachers can easily become traumatized by working with traumatized children, and administrators must strive to be understanding and compassionate to their staff. If faculty are treated poorly by the administration, through parallel process, the teachers will unknowingly disinvest in their students, teach half-heartedly, and otherwise be less emotionally available to their students.

In short, parallel process is the notion that when working with children exhibiting challenging behaviors, adults can unknowingly behave in similar, unhelpful ways to their superiors. In short, working with children suffering from low self-esteem can be stressful and parallel process is the uncanny experience of this stress becoming absorbed by, and/or exacerbated by, the system where the teachers, therapists, or child-care providers work.

Crisis De-Escalation, Secondary Factors Case Study: Harold's Hard Time

No one liked Harold. Other kids thought Harold was odd and stayed clear. He wasn't good at sports, and struggled with reading and writing. As an elementary school student, he isolated himself from his peers. Harold came from a large family and both of his parents were professionals. Harold didn't regularly bathe, his clothes were rarely clean, and he wore a winter coat inside the classroom most days.

Despite being bright, Harold spent years unavailable for an education. He appeared distracted by his own imagination and engaged in mischief rather than follow along in class. Illogical, terrifying worries about his health and his physical safety plagued him. For instance, he worried that his legs would randomly stop working and paralyze him, or that he would instantly become deaf. Harold hoarded food which he hid deep in his school desk. Most importantly, however, Harold was angry.

Harold's anger appeared different than other kids. He seemed almost constitutionally angry nearly all the time. Although rarely physically aggressive, Harold screamed profanity and insults at peers and teachers. One morning, his teacher asked him if he wanted a snack, and Harold angrily answered, "Go to hell!" The teacher wondered if she had angered him by asking about fruit. Harold burst into a rage calling her dreadful, sexually inappropriate names. Harold's angry outbursts appeared random. He would be sitting there quietly, then scream angrily at faculty members, seemingly without any identifiable provocation or "trigger." It was as if Harold's teacher had, in Harold's mind, become someone who had wronged him. Of course, Harold received consequences for his misconduct, but nothing seemed to help him change his behavior. Harold would also seem to forget why he received consequences. He would scream profanity, then seem to authentically forget what he had done.

Staff read *Reducing Anger and Violence in Schools* and tried talking to him about his anger, but processing didn't work. He accused the teachers of provoking him and fabricated reasons for his angry, verbal attacks. "I got mad because you called me gay," Harold angrily shouted.

Confused, the teacher pleaded, "I didn't mean to anger you, and I would never comment about your sexuality, Harold. I asked if you were ready to learn science." Sometimes Harold was very difficult to follow. Harold's teacher reached out to his family, but they were very difficult to contact. The school became increasingly concerned and made a referral to a psychiatrist that the district had previously worked with.

One day, Harold's behavior was particularly odd. He screamed that his teacher was a rapist, and that he didn't feel safe with her. Then he calmed and apologized. One of the school administrators asked to speak with Harold regarding his comment. The administrator explained that Harold would have to be suspended for his behavior, but during the conversation, Harold began cursing and accusing the administrator of things he hadn't done. The conversation went something like this:

Harold:	I hate you. You're an asshole.
Administrator:	Let's not talk until you're calm.
Harold:	Ok. I'm sorry. I'm ready now. I know what I said was bad. I'm sorry . . . but you're an asshole (screaming), and no one likes you. I hate you. No, sorry. Ok, I can do it now. I'm ready to talk. . . .
Administrator:	Ready to talk? Upset?
Harold:	I'm fine.
Administrator:	Ok. Harold, you called me some pretty bad names. What's up?
Harold:	What are you talking about? I would never call you names . . . but you're an asshole. . . .

The administrator was bewildered. After sitting with Harold, he felt like he had forgotten something important. It wasn't that the administrator couldn't handle Harold's behavior, it was as if he was in a fog. The administrator felt angry, disturbed, and confused. The administrator asked himself, "Did that really just happen?"

One day, Harold's teacher planned to attend a conference after work. The plan was that she would drive with colleagues, who also worked with Harold, to a nearby bus stop and take a charter bus into the city. The day turned out to be a difficult one for Harold. Following dismissal, the group of teachers drove to the bus station and on the drive began talking about Harold. Although the group arrived early for their trip, each teacher lost track of time in their conversation. The group dissociated. They arrived an hour early for their bus, but missed the boarding. Each teacher reported feeling overwhelmed and baffled, like time stood still. Each teacher also reported feeling disoriented.

The administrator met with the teachers. The administrator hypothesized that Harold's anger wasn't due to empathic failure, but was an emotion he manufactured to provide himself a sense of cohesion. Harold's anger may have been holding Harold together. It became clear that until someone could properly help Harold, his teachers required time to debrief, work as a team, and discuss possible parallel processes. That is, if there was a link between their experience with Harold and how they treated or were treated by the administration. They came to wonder if the unusual feelings they were experiencing were the same the terrible emotions that Harold battled. Maybe by experiencing these feelings, they were attempting to become closer to Harold. It also become clear that what Harold needed to succeed in school was different than what other students required. The teachers agreed to not try to "make" Harold into a typical student, and the administrator attempted to empathize with the team.

The team came to the realization that working with Harold was emotionally exhausting and left them feeling fragmented. No one individually could think straight, but as a team they carved time out of the day to process among themselves about Harold. Although Harold couldn't process his emotions, the team processed theirs. At the end of the school year, Harold continued to have difficulties, but because his teachers had time to talk about their own experiences with Harold, they all felt a little less crazy.

Discussion

This case study is not the typical de-escalation case study. Rather than focusing on the primary factor of self-awareness, it explored how a foundation of self-awareness was necessary for the team to process among themselves to better understand their experience working with Harold in an effort to manage a student with very challenging behaviors.

Clinical experience suggests that a crisis with a child can be de-escalated when adults observe their own emotional responses. This is because childhood behavior can be an attempt by the child to communicate difficult feeling states, and an engaged adult's self-aware response communicates understanding and caring that relieve the child's need to express feelings by acting out. This allows the child to feel understood, contains the emotion, and enables the child to change the emotional context and/or meaning of the experience. This work is difficult. The care provider must be authentic. Moreover, adults benefit when they work together as a team, have opportunities for debriefing, and are aware of parallel processing.

Learning Activity

Think of a recent crisis you've experienced with a student or child. What happened? Write a brief paragraph outlining the incident. Then, separately list your experience. What was your body communicating to you? What were you:

- Doing
- Thinking
- Feeling
- Sensing
- Hoping

If you wish, show your list to a trusted colleague. What does he or she experience during a crisis? Do you imagine that you are "sharing" the student's emotions?

Application Activity

Think about student or child you know well who suffers from behavioral difficulties. Think of the sorts of difficulties he or she has. Typically, students have the same sorts of difficulties that they repeat. When thinking of a particular student and his or her difficulty, dissect the functioning of the difficulty into two parts.

1. What powerful emotion do you believe that the behavior could be protecting the child from? Write your answer.
2. Can you imagine a way that the behavior could be an attempt at relatedness? That is, could the behavioral difficulty be an attempt for you, the adult, to understand something important about the child? Write your response.

    Adult debriefing, teamwork, and parallel process, the secondary factors in de-escalation, are vital components that enable adults to provide the best teaching or care to children. Have you ever experienced parallel process? Write a brief account of how a difficulty with a child seemed to spread to a difficulty within the system where you work or worked. What sort of measures do you believe could have been utilized to support you and your work with a challenging child?

Additional Resources

For the reader interested in a more comprehensive approach to de-escalation, I highly recommend contacting the Family Life Development Center at Cornell University. They have an outstanding Therapeutic Crisis Intervention program.

References

Benjamin, J. (2010). Can we recognize each other? Response to Donna Orange. *The International Association for Psychoanalytic Self Psychology, 5,* 244–256.

Bowen, M. (1974). *Toward the differentiation of self in one's family of origin.* New York, NY: J. Aronson.

Boyer, B., & Giovacchini, P. (1993). *Master clinicians in treating the regressed patient.* New York, NY: Jason Aronson.

Colvin, G., & Sugai, G. (1989). *Understanding and managing escalating behavior presentation.* Retrieved from http://www.pbis.org

Creswell, J. (1994). *Research design: Qualitative & quantitative approaches.* Thousand Oaks, CA: Sage Publications.

Devine, M. (2013). *The way of the SEAL: Think like an elite warrior to lead and succeed.* New York, NY: Reader's Digest.

Family Life Development Center. (2001). *Therapeutic crisis intervention: A crisis prevention and management system.* Ithaca, NY: Cornell University Press.

Goldenberg. I., & Goldenberg, H. (2004). *Family therapy: An overview* (6th ed.). Pacific Grove, CA: Thomson Brooks/Cole.

Kabat-Zinn, J., & Williams, M. (2013). *Mindfulness: Diverse perspectives on its meaning, origins, and applications.* New York, NY: Routledge Publishing.

McKay, M., Fanning, P., Paleg, K., & Landid, D. (1996). *When anger hurts your kids: A parent's guide.* Oakland, CA: New Harbinger Publications. Inc.

Mehrabian, A. (1981). *Silent messages; implicit communication of emotions and attitudes* (2nd ed.). Belmont, CA: Wadsworth Publishing.

Miller, J. (1996). *Using self psychology in child psychotherapy: The restoration of the child.* Lanham, England: Jason Aronson.

Nicholson, J., Perez, L., & Kurtz, J. (2019). *Trauma-informed practices for early childhood educators: Relationship-based approaches that support healing and building resilience in young children.* New York, NY: Routledge.

Russell, P. L. (2006). The theory of the crunch. *Smith College Studies in Social Work, 76*(1–2), 9–21.

Searles, H. (1955). The informational value of the supervisor's emotional experience. *Psychiatry, 18,* 135–146.

Small, R. (2001). *A hundred years of phenomenology: Perspectives on a philosophical tradition.* Burlington, VT: Ashgate.

Stolorow, R. (1999). The phenomenology of trauma and the absolutisms of everyday life: A personal journey. *Psychoanalytic Psychology, 16,* 464–468.

Stolorow, R. (2007). *Trauma and human existence.* New York, NY: Analytic Press.

Tufford, L., & Newman, P. (2010). Bracketing in qualitative research. *Qualitative Social Work, 0*(0), 1–17.

Watkins, C. E. Jr. (2012). Some thoughts about parallel process and psychotherapy supervision: When is a parallel just a parallel? *Psychotherapy Theory Research Practice Training, 49*(3), 344–346.

Watkins, C. E. Jr. (2017). Reconsidering parallel process in psychotherapy supervision: On parsimony, rival hypotheses, and alternate explanations. *Psychoanalytic Psychology, 34*(4), 506–515.

7 Understanding: High Self-Esteem

The previous five chapters of *Reducing Anger and Violence in Schools* have shown how angry, aggressive children are, for the most part, simply kids who have not been able to develop good enough self-esteem. Because self-esteem comes from meaningful relationships with special adults and not from a child's capabilities or accomplishments, children with low self-esteem were likely unable to idealize nurturing adults or feel connected to empathic grown-ups during early development. Children who do not receive empathic understanding as infants and toddlers may lash out later when they go to school. This is because these children can't tolerate all the big feelings that confront them in the schoolhouse. Without durable self-esteem, everyday frustrations morph into anger and possibly violence.

At a European conference on self-esteem, Michael Clifford, PhD, proposed that children need close, connected relationships so badly that when admirable grown-ups aren't available, kids use their imagination. They may attempt to have their psychological needs met through movies, television, and literature. Clifford believes that the most famous therapist of all, Sigmund Freud, attempted to have his boyish relational needs met by reading William Shakespeare. Ideally, children grow and mature through their meaningful associations with actual people, but because the need is so great they attempt to meet it creatively in the absence of available grown-ups.

When a like-minded adult is available to mirror a child and be idealized by them, self-esteem rises and the child is able to experience the admired adult as part of themselves, and a deep emotional connection or belonging then follows. As the child begins to feel that he or she belongs and is understood, anger subsides. Most of us have likely experienced this in our own lives. We internalize the people who were important in our development. We may have a wise elder—perhaps a parent, grandparent, professor, faith-based leader, or teacher—whose wisdom we can summon when needed. If so, that's because this wise person has psychologically become a part of us (McLean, 2007). This same process happens to a child when he or she absorbs the trusted adult into their character. This is made possible when the grown-up the child idealizes mirrors and emotionally connects with them, becoming a lasting part of the child's mind (Baker & Baker, 1987).

In short, once a child has psychologically grown up and developed a strong sense of self, they no longer need to idealize adults. They can have relationships that are more complex and not based primarily on meeting their developmental needs.

High Self-Esteem Enables Authentic Relationships

Although idealization is necessary during a certain part of a child's development, when relied upon without reflection or the ability to accept imperfection, idealization actually prevents authenticity and limits adult emotional connectedness. It may feel great for therapists, counselors, and teachers to be idealized. Some believe that the desire to be idealized is why many people enter the helping professions, and if they didn't want to be put on a pedestal, they probably wouldn't do as much good work (Wolf, 1988). However, when children grow past their need for sustained, unmodified idealization, the adults must also be open to a new type of relationship. That is not to say, however, that adults don't need to hold themselves to idealized standards of behavior, have an internal moral compass, or admire aspects of other adults. They do! But when children have high self-esteem, it becomes easier for them to "grow" out of this need for idealization and develop stronger, deeper, more complex peer relationships.

In comparison to children who have low self-esteem and unmet empathic needs, those with high self-esteem are better able to tolerate the disagreements and disappointments that are a natural part of authentic interactions and everyday life. Clinical wisdom suggests that people with a highly developed self-esteem are adept at building authentic relationships. In addition, they are also drawn to connect more deeply with others.

High Self-Esteem Allows Children to Grow Into Their Own Identity

Just as taking a child's perspective is vital, paradoxically, it can also prevent growth. In clinical settings, it can be tricky to determine how much someone needs the therapist to mirror them versus how much they can tolerate a different perspective. For example, we have all known someone who always

Figure 7.1

agreed with us. At first, it's great! We like Chinese food; they like Chinese food. We want to go to the movies; they want to go to the movies. But a relationship with someone like this turns stifling quickly! If a person is always agreeable, then there's no discussion, no learning from them, no seeing his or her perspective, and thus the desire for authentic interaction is frustrated.

The person who always agrees with us may also idealize us and thus lacks interest in actually wanting to know who we really are. Of course, this kind of behavior is usually indicative of people with low-esteem and may be a result of their unmet idealization, empathy, or closeness needs. Their agreeable behavior is an attempt to meet those needs.

When children have high self-esteem, on the other hand, they are able to have their own opinions and authentically engage with others. They no longer need to idealize or demand that others only admire them or empathize with them. They have a sense of identity, are not forced to agree with others, and can truly compromise.

Building Self-Esteem in the Conflicted Child Case Study: Tyrone the Cyclone

Tyrone, a fifth-grade student, seemed to have two moods: happy and angry. Almost every day he strolled into the classroom in high spirits. Most mornings he was usually the first one to arrive. He was happy and thrived on the positive, individual attention from his teacher. However, as soon the bell rang to start the school day, Tyrone started pacing. Pacing escalated to running, and by midmorning, Tyrone was running down the halls of the school. When asked to take a break in the Chill Zone, Tyrone refused and readied himself for combat. The boy who was happy and calm hours before was angrily defiant. If his teacher tried to escort him to the Chill Zone, he would scream, kick, slap, and punch. This pattern repeated itself most school days.

During eating times, free times, or when Tyrone was asked to help out with chores or errands in the school building, he was happy and content. As soon as school work demands were placed on him, even listening during "read aloud" times (when a teacher reads from a book to the class), he became agitated and disruptive. This behavior existed despite the fact that Tyrone was a bright student who struggled a little with math but was a strong reader.

Tyrone's classroom teacher, Becky, was perplexed by his pattern of ups and downs throughout the school day. Even though the classroom had a point system on which all students were rewarded for cooperation, calm/safe body, and respectfulness every half hour block, this had little effect on Tyrone. The school provided him weekly counseling, and that too failed. Tyrone immediately disliked his counselor. Despite her efforts, counseling wasn't a good fit. Becky knew Tyrone needed something different. The behavior plans that were supposed to work didn't.

She decided to ask Tyrone when he came in first thing in the morning, when it was just the two of them, what he needed to be successful. To really listen to him and try her best to understand, Becky asked him why he was having such a hard time at school. Tyrone's answer was, "I don't know." The more Becky inquired, the more annoyed he became.

Becky decided to try a different approach. Tyrone clearly enjoyed doing physical work. He seemed to feel competent and capable when asked to do such tasks. In fact, he seemed to take pride in his ability to carry heavy boxes, deliver messages, or clean bulletin boards. He also enjoyed helping out with kindergarten students who behaved much like him at times. It was remarkable for Becky to see Tyrone telling a five-year-old the same kinds of things that she told him about regulating his emotions and problem-solving.

Becky built "Helper" blocks into Tyrone's day, during which the two of them would do jobs and complete errands around the school, often helping other teachers or students as part of the process. Becky hypothesized that Tyrone's emotions were too strong to just sit and talk about. She thought that maybe they could have more open conversations while working and not obviously talking about his feelings.

In no time, Tyrone started to open up with Becky while they ran their errands. He talked about his father who had died unexpectedly two years before. He talked about how much he hated his mother because she was always commenting that he was too fat and needed to eat less and lose weight. He also talked about how much he worried about his mother and her smoking, and how mad it made him that she didn't take better care of herself. The list went on. All these worries and concerns poured out of Tyrone.

The more Tyrone spoke to Becky and others during his chores, the more he settled in the classroom. He still had worries and regularly reported fights and arguments at home, but his school behavior improved. Eventually, Tyrone was able to sit during read-aloud periods and attempted to do his school work. He tolerated transitions from eating or free time to classroom time better. He was able to willingly walk to the Chill Zone when he needed to sit away from other students in order to concentrate. Tyrone still had rough days, but he no longer went berserk. He was able to engage in his academic responsibilities and misbehaved less.

Tyrone's teacher, Becky, saw that the usual strategies weren't helping. She knew Tyrone had a lot on his plate at home and that he brought his troubles to school. She also recognized that he couldn't tolerate the typical sit-and-talk counseling and that positive rewards didn't seem to work.

Initially, she thought to simply ask him what was wrong. This backfired. She learned that by asking him, she was communicating that she didn't really know him. This was awful for Tyrone because he was wishing, like so many children, that his teacher could read his mind—her questions reminded him that she wasn't really connected to him. Using the approach she had learned in *Reducing Anger and Violence in Schools*, she attempted to take an empathic stance and to establish herself as a role model Tyrone could look up to. To do this, Becky had to ask herself, "How would Tyrone want to be approached, and how will I need to treat him for him to have a healthy idealization of me?"

Discussion

Through her growing connection with Tyrone, Becky tried to understand what he really wanted and needed in order to build his feelings of self-worth. She playfully worked with his strengths. Tyrone liked helping, so she invited him to be a helper. This was real empathy in action. By considering Tyrone's perspective, Becky was able to tailor an approach that worked best for him. By taking an empathic approach she further strengthened their connection, which encouraged Tyrone to be more vulnerable and open up to her more. Her hunch paid off. Tyrone became more talkative while doing work together. The more competent he felt by being entrusted with these helping activities, the less wild he became. His self-esteem increased. The jobs also provided him a place of belonging. He had a way to contribute to his school. With that, Tyrone felt better about himself at school. He became important and subsequently was better able to tolerate the academic demands of his school day. With Becky's creativity, Tyrone calmed his inner and outer storm.

In conclusion, it's important to remember that durable self-esteem is not derived from what a person possesses or their aptitude and accomplishments. The ability to control frustration, i.e., reduce childhood anger and subsequent violence, depends upon building self-esteem in children who suffer with a low self-worth. Moreover, children with high self-esteem possess it because of the important relationships they have assimilated into their personality. High self-esteem occurs when the child has the opportunity to absorb empathic role models and is in an environment that cherishes him or her.

Learning Activity

Think of someone you consider to have high self-esteem.

1. What type of relationships does this person have with other people?
2. Are other people drawn to them?
3. What kinds of things do you admire about them?
4. Do they have standards you find yourself idealizing?

Write a paragraph describing your particular relationship with this person and what they have taught you about your own self-esteem.

Application Activity

Think about your students, clients, or patients who are doing well. Do their peers recognize their functioning? Choose one student and write a paragraph about your observations regarding his or her peer relationships.

1. Do their peers admire them?
2. Is the student able to show empathy toward his or her classmates?
3. Does he or she belong to a pro-social, positive peer group?

The purpose of the activity isn't to judge another, but to enable a better understanding of the Healing the Self model so that it can be successfully applied.

References

Baker, H.S., & Baker, M.N. (1987). Heinz Kohu's self psychology: An overview. *American Journal of Psychiatry*, *144*(1), 1–9. doi: 10.1176/aip.144.1.1

McLean, J. (2007). Psychotherapy with a narcissistic patient using Kohut's self psychology model. *Psychiatry*, *4*(10), 40–47.

Wolf, E. (1988). *Treating the self: Elements of clinical self psychology*. New York, NY: Guilford Press.

8   Healing the Self—An Evidence-Based Practice

As has been emphasized in previous chapters, experience shows that relationships have the power to heal or hurt. Finding solace in relationships and/or becoming frustrated or angry with others defines the human experience. The children featured in the case studies in this book have more than amply illustrated this. The notion that empathic therapists deeply understand children is not new, but providing non-therapists these tools is very new indeed. As we have seen in the previous chapters, the Healing the Self model teaches us that adults who care about children, including teachers, counselors, and other caregivers, can create the kind of relationships that may heal many of the hurts and disappointments that angry children have experienced in other relationships in their lives.

Up to this point, *Reducing Anger and Violence in Schools* has focused on the basic relational elements of the Healing the Self model—idealization, empathy, and belonging—and the practical application of these elements by educators and counselors in their relationships with troubled children. The book explains the model in terms that can help all adults more readily integrate the complex concepts taught herein. In this chapter, we dig deeper into the science behind Healing the Self and explore the meaning of evidence-based practice.

It is the role of science to explore the world we live in. To do this, good science observes both subjective and objective data. Subjective data is personal and thus variable, whereas objective data is based on replicable facts. Both subjective and objective information are important, and good science observes both types of data (Solms, 2015). As we define and demonstrate how Healing the Self is a member of the family of evidence-based practices, we explore both subjective experience and objective facts for a comprehensive investigation of behavior.

Subjective Experience

Your subjective experience is vital. There are two basic questions that can be used to ascertain your subjective experience of the model. First, does this developmental model appear reasonable and match with your subjective experience? As the reader, does the model, or parts of it, match your experience as a child, adult, and possibly as a parent? Have you experienced that children require admirable, empathic adults, and a sense of belonging to be at their best? If your personal experience or your observations of children don't confirm this model, then it calls into question its validity (Solms, 2015).

Second, does it pass the "Grandmother Test"? Although rarely written about in the scientific literature, the Grandmother Test was drilled into practicum students studying pediatric neuropsychology at the Geisel School of Medicine at Dartmouth College. The test is simple. If your grandmother (or a reasonable grandmother you know) wouldn't approve of something you wanted to do or say to a child, don't do it. This is a very personal, subjective test that actually has two parts. First, do you believe that your grandmother would find aspects of the Healing the Self model harmful to her grandchild or other kids? Second, would your grandmother believe that it is reasonable to help children feel less angry and behave less violently by encouraging:

- Children to admire appropriate role models
- Adults to try their best to deeply understand children
- That troubled children are included, cherished, and develop a sense of belonging

If you find this model doesn't pass this simple, but important test, then don't use Healing the Self. Moreover, if your beliefs (or your grandmother's) concerning child-rearing counter aspects of this model, then again, don't use it. As this chapter later demonstrates, for a practice to be considered a member of the family of evidence-based practice, it must include subjective experience. In practical terms, the model has to make sense to you and your grandmother.

In the development of the Healing the Self model, research into adults' subjective experience played a crucial role. To explore the experience of adults using this model, teachers, counselors, principals, special education administrators, pediatricians, varying types of child therapists, and parents were asked the following opened-ended questions during conferences and workshops held throughout the U.S. and in Europe:

- Who was important in your development?
- Why was that person important in your development?

Without exception, every respondent who was asked named an individual who they admired, who seemed to understand them deeply, and/or who assisted them in developing a sense of belonging. One respondent elaborated that he couldn't admire his parents for a particular reason, so he found a home in his family's church. He admired his minister who was kind and empathic towards him. Subjective experience, though not replicable in the same way as objective data, is important.

It is critical to explore these questions and our subjective experience of them with any developmental model that we plan on using with children. Doing so enables us not only to understand the working parts of a model like Healing the Self, but promotes confidence in it. Most simply, because we were all kids once, we should be able to answer the question: Does this model seem right to us as people?

Objective Science

Objective data is comprised of what we know through science. There are two primary ways that scientists collect facts regarding children: by studying the brain and through careful observation of child behavior. Neuroscience provides us a map of the brain, which provides us information regarding the physical genesis of behavior, while careful observation enables us to make inferences regarding external behavior (Solms, 2015). The next section briefly outlines neuroscience and behavioral observation to provide a backdrop for better understanding evidence-based practice and the basis of Healing the Self.

Neuroscience

Neuroscience has located the parts of the brain responsible for the foundation of self-esteem. These brain structures are the physical building blocks for these interpersonal functions. The human brain is composed of millions of neurons, which are shaped like trees. Neurons are electrically active cells which talk to each other through the transmission of impulses. Neurons connect with other neurons forming large networks that are devoted to specific tasks. If neurons can be considered trees, then these networks can be considered super dense forests (Seung, 2012).

Our actions, thoughts, and feelings arise from the activity of specific neural networks of the brain. We can measure the activity of these neural networks through the use of functional Magnetic Resonance Imaging (fMRI). fMRI machines measure the activity of neurons in the brain and allow scientists to create brain maps. For instance, when we look at other people's faces during an fMRI scan, a specific part of the brain called the *primary face area* activates (Kanwisher, Stanley, & Harris, 1999). In contrast, when people remember the birth of their child, a much different area of the brain becomes active, the *autobiographic memory network* (Spreng & Grady, 2010). There are also regions of the brain devoted to movement, vision, hearing, sensation, decision-making and many other mental faculties—all these have been discovered using fMRI.

In the late 1990s, scientists placed volunteers in fMRI machines and asked them to view pictures of their friends while thinking about their friends' feelings and actions. Scientists were very surprised to discover that specific networks in the brain activated when volunteers thought about other people.

This led scientists to construct maps of the brain networks that are involved in social thinking. These areas were dubbed the *social cognitive network*. Over many studies, it became apparent that the *social cognitive network* is one of the largest networks of the brain and involves many brain regions including parts of the frontal, temporal, and parietal lobes of the brain. The human brain is specifically designed to think about other people.

Over the past 20 years, scientists have used a variety of research tools such as fMRI, positron emission tomography (PET), and electroencephalogram (EEG) to study the composition and activity of the human *social cognitive network*. One of the most important discoveries has been the recording of special brain cells called *mirror neurons*. When we think about reaching for a cup of coffee, an area of the brain becomes active called the *primary motor area*. Conversely, when we watch another person reach for a cup of coffee, a separate area of the brain becomes active called the *primary sensory area*. This was exciting because previously, scientists thought that motor areas were very distinct from sensory areas.

Scientists working at the University of Parma in Italy discovered that certain neurons in the brains of monkeys became active both when the monkey reached for a food pellet and when the monkey watched another monkey reach for a food pellet (di Pellegrino, Fadiga, Fogassi, Gallese, & Rizzolatti, 1992). These special neurons appeared to have properties of both motor and sensory neurons, i.e., they tended to mirror something we observe into our own actions. Mirror neurons were first discovered in primates and subsequently have been discovered in people. The discovery of *mirror neurons* transformed how scientists thought about the way the human brain worked. It became apparent that our brain is hard-wired to imitate the behaviors and actions of people around us. Mirror neurons are the neuroanatomical foundation for empathy; in others words, our human brains are designed for empathy.

In 2003, Dr. Rebecca Saxe discovered a very special area of the brain called the Temporo-Parietal Junction (TPJ) while working at MIT labs. Using an fMRI scanner, Dr. Saxe was able to show that this area becomes active only when we think about the mental states of other people, and does not become active when we simply look at other people (Saxe & Kanwisher, 2003). She reasoned that the TPJ is specifically designed to think about the contents of another person's thoughts. This ability—called the *theory of mind*—is the ability to attribute mental states such as beliefs, desires, emotions, and knowledge to others. Scientists now believe that a specific neural network, which includes the TPJ but also parts of the frontal and parietal lobes, allows us to incorporate other people's thoughts and actions into our own behavior. As with mirror neurons, scientific evidence supports the idea that our brain is hard-wired to think about other people. *Theory of mind* and mirror neurons are the neuroanatomic basis that enables people to imagine what another person is doing, feeling, and thinking, as well as use our guess regarding someone else's experience to guide us.

In addition to mirror neurons and the TPJ, scientists discovered that certain regions of the brain that register feeling physical pain become active in certain social situations. In 2004, Naomi Eisenberger and Matt Lieberman placed volunteers in fMRI machines and asked them to play a video game called Cyberball (Eisenberger & Lieberman, 2004). In Cyberball, a person is required to pass a ball to two other people. At a certain point in the game, the two other people in the game pass the ball to each other and exclude the volunteer in the fMRI scanner. Cyberball, a form of digital catch, was designed to mimic social exclusion. The person "playing" Cyberball thinks that the two other real people are excluding him or her.

In the fMRI scanner, it became apparent that social exclusion activated a region in the brain called the *anterior cingulate gyrus*, a region which also gets activated when we feel physical pain (Eisenberger, 2012). Scientists now believe that social exclusion activates specific pain networks in the brain, similar to networks that are activated when a person perceives physical pain. Being left out hurts just the same as breaking your leg. The need to belong is powerful, and if not met, results in real pain which can be visualized in the brain using fMRI. Just as with mirror neurons and the TPJ, activation of the anterior cingulate gyrus during social exclusion provides evidence that the human brain is hard-wired for social belonging. In short, neuroscience has now pinpointed the areas of the brain that allow for empathy and the human need to belong.

Neuroscience remains in its infancy, and as we continue to explore the brain with fMRI and other emerging technologies, researchers will be better able to understand the neuroanatomy of our interpersonal needs. Perhaps future investigators will better understand the process by which neurons communicate, pinpoint brain regions responsible for idealization, and enable more effective biological interventions.

Human Behavior

The other form of objective data is careful observation. Because brain science remains in its infancy, investigators usually rely on observing human behavior first, then making inferences from those observations. This is the current method of gaining empirical, objective information about our world in the field of psychology.

The Healing the Self approach is an evidence-based practice grown from an empirically supported scientific tradition. But what does it mean for a treatment or an approach to be evidence-based, and why does this matter to educators and others in terms of adopting the Healing the Self model? The following sections of this chapter define the characteristics needed for an approach to be evidence-based, summarizes our current understanding of how psychological change occurs, explains why the Healing the Self model fits within the community of evidence-based practices, and discusses how it works with other approaches.

What Makes a Practice Evidence-Based?

In the 1990s, a group of British physicians—David Sacket, William Rosenberg, Muir Gray, Brian Haynes, and Scott Richardson—wondered if engaging in medicine in the same old ways could perhaps mean they were missing something. They entered into a scientific conversation regarding how best to practice medicine and questioned whether following research and training alone was enough to most effectively help their patients. Their discussions led to them writing a now famous paper, "Evidence-based Medicine: What It Is and What It Isn't," in which they proposed the idea that physicians needed to use good judgment, listen to their patients' point of view, and utilize the best research to guide their practice (Sackett, Rosenberg, Gray, Haynes, & Richardson, 1996). This concept of "evidence-based" practice is now used worldwide and in many other service fields including nursing, counseling, and education, all of which strive to make sure their patients, clients, or students are receiving the highest level of professional care or instruction. Subsequently, the American Psychological Association (APA) developed their own task force to encourage psychologists to also adopt evidence-based approaches in their own work as therapists and researchers. The APA's task force (2005) further elaborated the three elements required for a treatment to be considered evidence-based:

- Good judgment
- Inclusion of patients' insights and preferences
- Unbiased, empirical research

Because the Healing the Self model focuses on each of these three components of an evidence-based approach, it too is a member of the large community of evidence-based practices. The model doesn't offer new ideas in and of itself, but rather is a collection of validated, relationship-based psychotherapy approaches made available to non-therapists in a new way. Moreover, the model relies on and emphasizes the use of the three standards described above. One way of understanding the principle behind evidence-based approaches, and how the Healing the Self model uses them, is to think of evidence-based practice as three different groups of people working together: practitioners, clients, and researchers.

Practitioners (Therapists and Teachers)

Evidence-based practice requires good judgment by the practitioners using the approach. "Evidence-based medicine is not 'cookbook' medicine" (Sackett et al., 1996, p. 72). It uses the best available information paired with the clinician's best judgment. In *Reducing Anger and Violence in Schools*, "evidence-based" means that adults using this model are regularly questioning how well their experience with a child fits with the framework of the model and whether is seems to be working. They apply the model, but they also listen to their best judgment based on past experience and common sense working with children. They modify their approach with the model as they go based on their conclusion about what is working and what is not.

Teaching requires flexibility, fast thinking, and a steady focus. Every teacher, or anyone who works with children, knows that no lesson plan survives contact with the students. The best plans serve only as flexible guidelines in often chaotic classrooms. In the same light, it's imperative in this model that teachers do not blindly strive to be idealized, empathic, and develop a sense of belonging without those efforts being grounded in their experience and feedback from the child and the classroom in the moment. In teaching, students require different approaches, and it's ultimately up to the teacher to strive to find what works to foster a connection with an individual student. In the context of Healing the Self, evidence-based practice includes using one's best judgment and experience. Evidence-based practice for the Healing the Self model is not intended to diminish the professional freedom required to teach, treat, or otherwise help children.

Clients (Students or Patients)

Evidence-based practice means a commitment to humbly ask for and heed the input of the people that we are striving to serve. It incorporates subjective experience: people's likes, dislikes, thoughts, feelings, and opinions. Too often, adults do not seek the guidance of children in our interventions, whether they are in schools, hospitals, or clinics. Typically, the adults apply the treatments and, if they don't work, they assume there is something else wrong with the child or that there has been a mismatch between child and treatment. Sadly, adults rarely ask the child if what the grown-ups are doing is helping. By actively listening to and inquiring about what is working and what is helpful to students, adults are engaging the principle of empathy; they are striving to understand the child's point of view. Not only can this be effective in its own right, but the child's responses are a critical component to any evidence-based practice.

Researchers

For research to be considered credible, replicable findings must be published in peer-reviewed academic journals. In the simplest sense, researchers carefully observe behaviors, develop hypotheses, and then attempt to test the hypotheses. In regards to human behavior, published empirical research overwhelmingly supports the notion that relationships can heal. But how do we know? Psychologists have worked hard over the years to understand how to help people and identify the factors that aid them in getting better. The history of psychological exploration (or research) demonstrates why we know that special relationships can be curative. This section outlines the Common Factors research that identifies that it is the relationship that heals. It then further demonstrates that the core features of Healing the Self fit within the family of empirically supported, psychodynamic treatment approaches.

Common Factors

In 1936, psychologist, therapist, and professor Saul Rosenzweig investigated why psychotherapy seemed to work, and what the common factors were among helpful therapy approaches. His research discovered specific relational ingredients that were common among many effective forms of psychotherapy. These ingredients include therapeutic teamwork, empathy, expectations, cultural flexibility, and therapists' overall skill (Rosenzweig, 1936). He began to hypothesize that maybe these factors, all of which are relational, are what help the client; that it is the therapeutic relationship itself that helps people when they go to a therapist, rather than any specific thing the therapist says or does.

Seventy-five years later, the APA developed a task force to better understand what helps people achieve good mental health and what doesn't. John Norcross and Bruce Wampold, two leading psychology researchers who study what helps people in psychotherapy and what doesn't, examined multiple patterns of findings across collections of studies, and similar to Rosenzweig, found that common relationship factors within a healing relationship itself accounted for growth. "The therapy relationship makes substantial and constant contributions to psychotherapy outcome independent of the specific type of treatment" (Norcross & Wampold, 2011, p. 98). Rita Ardito and Daniela Rabellino (2011), researchers in the field of psychology, also found that the connection between therapist and client predicts if the therapy will be helpful. In 2015, Wampold revisited the therapeutic relationship and the notion of these common factors. His most recent research further advocates that common relationship factors accounted for much of the benefit of successful psychotherapy (Wampold, 2015). In short, science repeatedly tells us that it's the relationship itself that heals! The Healing the Self model incorporates this evidence-based research into the approach; its principles are grounded in the evidence that indicates the relationship is what can make a huge difference in childhood development. Psychology overwhelmingly supports that what "cures" people is the bond between humans, not the "interventions" that are applied.

Empirically Supported

Using meta-analysis, a method of examining the results of many studies at once, Jonathan Shedler demonstrated that relationship-based (psychodynamic) treatment approaches were empirically supported by science. "Effect size of psychodynamic therapies are as large as those reported for other therapies that have been actively promoted as 'empirically supported' and 'evidence based.'" (Shedler, 2010, p. 98.) Moreover, Shedler writes, the effects of dynamic therapy last even months and years after the end of treatment. This is perhaps because the client absorbed the healthy aspects of the therapist-client relationship and increased their self-esteem.

The hallmarks of psychodynamic therapies are the notions of the unconscious and transference. In the simplest sense, the unconscious is the idea that people are not truly aware of why they behave the way they do, and that what drives human behavior is, to an extent, unknown. Transference is the idea that people project emotions and emotional needs onto the therapist. To the reader familiar with therapy from a psychodynamic perspective, idealization and feeling similar (also called twinship) are types of transference. Within modern psychodynamic traditions, many of the authors cited in *Reducing Anger and Violence in Schools*, including Heinz Kohut, Anna Orenstein, Richard Geist, and other thinkers, have all written extensively regarding self-esteem and empathy from a psychodynamic perspective. These thinkers focus on self-esteem and can be referred to as Self Psychologists. In short, the structure of Healing the Self heavily borrows from the broad category of empirically validated psychodynamic tradition.

For a practice to be evidence-based it must take into account clients', teachers', and patients' preferences, the professional's judgment, and unbiased research. Beginning in the 1930s and continuing to the present-day, empirical research has overwhelmingly supported that it is the relationship, as opposed to any specific intervention, that accounts for psychological change. Furthermore, idealization, feeling similar, and empathic understanding are features that fit within the family of empirically supported, psychodynamic treatment approaches.

How Healing the Self Works With Other Approaches

Because relationships, in one form or another, accompany every interaction with children, the Healing the Self model dovetails easily and well with other approaches. The model is an invitation for adults to hold key concepts in their minds which directly influence relationships when working with children. It does not dictate specific behavioral techniques or intervention scripts (for instance, when Johnny does *that, everyone says this*). Of course, adults meriting respect and offering empathic inquiries are a form of intervention, in and of themselves. An adult can strive to be authentic, provide structure, be empathic, and foster a sense of belonging while using any combination of disciplinary approaches, reward systems, social skills training, mindfulness-based practices, or token economies. In this sense, the model capitalizes on the common relationship factors that precipitate emotional growth.

Limitations to the Healing the Self Model

Despite being evidence-based and research-driven, the Healing the Self model, like all approaches, will sometimes fail. There are many reasons for this, but one reason revolves around the adult's fidelity to the model. It may be very difficult for adults to follow the model closely. First, the adults working with troubled children may not want to feel feelings. Second, adults may need to be taken care of themselves. Adults, due to their own histories and traumas, may not be available to provide the attunement that a child with low self-esteem needs. That is, the adult may not be at his or her best and operating at their full capacity to take the child's perspective. Instead, the adult may demand that the child take *their* perspective and therefore blur the generational boundaries that need to exist between adults and children.

It's best to think of children and adults together while accounting for the complex web of needs, wants, fears, and aspirations that everyone brings to and experiences in a family, school, or therapeutic environment. Models, even this one, can be dangerous whenever an adult puts the model before his own experience with the child. Although Healing the Self strives to cultivate empathic sensitivity, even that practice can be problematic if done thoughtlessly. Let's now take a closer look at two of the reasons why this model may fail.

Adults Don't Want to Feel Feelings

Helping children build a sense of self can be exhausting. This is because many children have limited insight into why they act the way they do and have yet to develop an age-appropriate ability to understand, feel, and ultimately let go of unpleasant emotions. Put simply, children with a low sense of self often attempt to make others feel their negative emotions for them. This is because a strong sense of self enables people to psychologically survive difficult feelings. For those with low self-esteem, uncomfortable feelings are erroneously thought of as dangerous and overwhelming to experience.

Figure 8.1

Figure 8.2

Because the child can't authentically experience these feelings directly, they give them to others. In this light, the misery is contagious. It is as if these children are playing "Hot Potato" with their emotions. They want to quickly give these terrible feelings to someone else before they are burned by them.

For instance, when a child feels weak, he or she may provoke an adult into feeling angry, aggravated, confused, or weak themselves. Thus, those working with these children are likely to feel irritated, frustrated, and angry.

It is natural, even expected, for invested adults working with children to periodically feel provoked, annoyed, or worse by children's behaviors. While it is unacceptable for these feelings to influence the adults' judgment or actions, the adults must be able to feel these emotions in order to continually invest in a child's success. If these feelings are too much for the adults to bear, they may tune out, give up, attempt to ignore problems, half-heartedly follow through with their efforts, or unknowingly sabotage the child's growth (Ornstein, 2017). When adults flee their own negative reactions to children it prevents the adult and the child from experiencing emotional closeness. The child may still admire the adult, and the adult may understand the child's perspective, but if the adult doesn't or can't help the child metabolize the entire spectrum of his or her emotions, the child won't be able to develop his or her self-esteem. Of course, sometimes adults feel angry because of the child's failure to empathize with them. How many of us have become angry with children because they just didn't understand how much we cared for them and wanted them to succeed?

Adults working with troubled children must be able to recognize when kids vex them, survive their own negative feelings, and prevent those negative feelings from tainting their judgment. Adults who use this model generally agree that helping others emotionally grow is exhausting. One way to reinvigorate oneself is to be part of a processing group that enables the adults to talk about the struggles and victories of working with challenging children. Adults working in this model may also benefit from engaging in their own emotional supports (support groups, faith-based organizations,

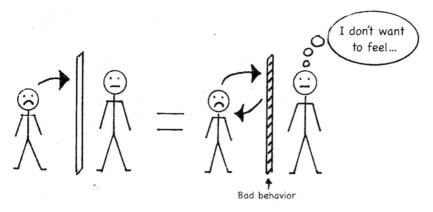

Figure 8.3

and counseling). This is important because without reflective practice, it becomes quite difficult to see a child with behavioral problems very clearly and to determine who is who in the encounter. Adults can practice reflection by simply asking themselves, "Is it the child behaving poorly, or am I having a bad day and am therefore overly sensitive to the child's behavior?"

Generational Boundaries

Children need adults to be real with them, but they also require authenticity without the loss of generational boundaries. That is, children need some hierarchy in a world that they are not yet privileged to join. Children require that the adults in their lives do not abdicate their adultness by blurring or ignoring the line between child and adult. This relational mistake most often comes in one of two guises: either the adult may himself act like a child (for example, by entering into power struggles with the child), or the adult may instead treat the child as an adult peer (for example, telling the child personal secrets or expecting him to equally contribute to his rearing). Children with a low sense of self particularly require strict generational boundaries, but they also need their behavior to be meaningful and to authentically affect the adults in their life. Adults around children need to feel but not completely lose themselves in the child's perspective.

Being aware of the reasons why the Healing the Self model sometimes doesn't work is important for educators, counselors, and others who are attempting to help children overcome anger and aggression. It is important to note, however, that when questions of not wanting to feel feelings with children or generational boundaries are challenged, all is not lost. When these things occur, the adult must be open to the misstep and simply readjust. In some schools of therapy, these mistakes or therapist enactments are considered inevitable and may even be necessary.

Future Research

The Healing the Self model is an innovative approach to using established ideas. In this way, it's unique because it introduces evidence-based therapeutic approaches to non-therapists in the novel setting of a school. As has been previously noted, its aim is to make evidence-based, relationship practices accessible to teachers, school counselors, principals, others who work with children, and, of course, parents. Because the model is both new and very old, future opportunities exist for investigators to further explore and compare this model to others, as well as to further dissect this approach to better understand which components are most useful or how its components can be further enhanced.

Neuroscience has made leaps and bounds, and perhaps future tools will allow us to better map and understand, at a physical level, the changes in the brain that occur when children increase their self-esteem. Moreover, as more schools adopt Healing the Self, greater opportunities will emerge to measure its effectiveness. Although specific research designs lay outside the scope of this chapter, future investigations could measure the use of this model not only in regards to reducing behavioral difficulties such as aggressive and/or violent behavior, but also in relation to academic performance. Science is a process and developing studies takes time. As more school systems adopt this model, rich opportunities will emerge for future investigators to assess the Healing the Self model as an independent treatment intervention.

Summary

An evidence-based approach requires a mix of good judgment, accounting for the patient's input and preferences, and unbiased research. Evidence-based approaches represent the ideal of combining professional judgment and knowledge with patient or student input in a collaborative effort to achieve healing and wellness. These elements of an evidence-based approach are the bedrock of the Healing the Self model. The model, at its core, encourages adults to use their best judgment and listen to and take an empathic stance.

Discussion

Science is a disciplined exploration. It requires investigating objective and subjective material. For a treatment to be considered a member of the family of evidence-based therapies, it requires incorporating the objective (replicable research), the clinician's judgment, and the subjective preferences of the patient. It is essential that the patient's preferences be accounted for and considered.

Evidence-Based Practice Case Study: Sally's Choice

Sally looked out an antique window in a restored farmhouse atop a hill in a residential treatment center. She felt defeated. She had entered treatment six weeks ago, hoping that fresh air and a slower pace would liberate her from her overbearing sense of sadness.

Sally dreamed of being a writer. She graduated from a competitive university and rather than entering the workforce upon graduation, returned home to her middle-class family. She was lonely. At home, her depressed mood increased. She tried seeing a therapist, but that didn't seem to help her. Her physician prescribed her an antidepressant medication, which also appeared ineffective. Weeks turned to months, and Sally's misery became a constant, intractable force in her life.

Sally wanted a change and admitted herself to an outdoor-themed treatment center hundreds of miles away from her urban home. At the center, she dutifully followed the treatment program regiment. She hiked when she was supposed to hike, bicycled when the group mountain biked, and attended yoga and mindfulness classes without complaint. She never missed a scheduled activity, made friends, and got along well with everyone.

The center took a holistic treatment approach. Clients were provided individual therapy, a vast selection of outdoor activities, and once weekly process-based group therapy. In individual therapy sessions, clients learned new adaptive skills to help them navigate the symptoms of their difficulties. Individual therapists often gave homework which corresponded to a treatment manual that clients worked on throughout their stay.

Conversely, the group therapy was process-based. Process-based group therapy is a therapeutic approach where, rather than the therapist teaching a specific skill or leading a topic, participants are encouraged to say whatever comes to mind. In a process group, the group leader simply facilitates the conversation and encourages the group members to be increasingly vulnerable (Yalom, 2005). In this form of therapy, difficulties between group members emerge and group members learn how to listen, confront, and ultimately heal each other.

In Sally's group, twelve members met weekly with a therapist. During session, members were invited to draw or doodle. During the last few minutes of the group, members were invited to show the group their drawings and discuss their meaning. This enabled clients who were less verbal to participate. Sally never missed a group.

In group, she generally sat quietly. She drew simple drawings. As was the custom, she showed them to the group, but refrained from discussing them. In one group, Sally had just returned from a difficult family phone call. She was disappointed. Her father had completely misunderstood her and the good advice her therapist gave her backfired. It was difficult for Sally to talk in the group. She shut herself down, saying that what she had to say wasn't worth the group members' time. A very talkative group member immediately filled the silence, discussing his experience on a recent canoeing trip. One of the group members politely attempted to refocus the group on Sally. Sally just shook her head "No."

In the following three weeks, Sally attended each group in silence. Simultaneously, Sarah's private practice grew, and she resigned from the center. In the final group meeting, Sarah told each member that if they wished, she would say goodbye in a private session. Sally bashfully asked her for a private goodbye on the last day.

Sally sat down across from Sarah in a private room, the hum of a sound machine protecting them both. Then Sarah began.

Sarah: Sally it's been great getting to know you. Thank you for attending our group. I wish you the best of luck. . . .

Sally: Yeah, thanks. . . . What would you say if your patient had high suicidal ideation?

Sarah: Are you telling me you want to die?

Sally: No. I have no plan, and no, I do not want to kill myself. But, if someone did, what would you say?

Sarah: Are you telling me you are going to kill yourself?

Sally: No.

Sarah: Well, when you're treating suicide, it all depends on the patient's age. If it's a kid, then it's easy to treat. I just say you are not allowed to do it, and you have to follow the rules, so that's that. If it's a grown-up, then it's different.

Sally: Ok, what if it was an adult like me?

Sarah: Oh, that's totally different.

Sally: What would you say?

Sarah: Are you telling me something?

Sally: No.

Sarah: If I'm working with a grown-up like you, I know exactly what I would say.

Sally: What?

Sarah: Oh, I'd say you are allowed to kill yourself, but not because of something I said.

Sally: What! How is that ok? So, if someone dies it's not on your conscience. That's not right.

Sarah: Yeah, you can kill yourself, but not because of me.

Sally: That's not right, you wouldn't say that.

Sarah: Yes. I would.

Sally: How is that therapy?

Sarah: Let me explain. The idea is that if I was working with someone like you, I would try to become as close to you as possible. I would try to read your mind, almost become one; be so attuned that you wouldn't know where you stopped and I began. I would try my best to simply really know and understand you. To sit with you and listen deeply. But I would inevitably mess up. I would say the wrong thing. Something stupid. Then, I would need you to forgive me. That would be the therapy. Because, maybe, if you forgave me, then

you could forgive yourself and not want to die so badly. Forgiving
me would be forgiving you.

Sally: (Bursting into tears.) This is the sort of therapy I need. I want to talk
to you longer.

Sarah: We've got time, let's figure it out together. I'm protecting this time
and we're talking about it. . . .

At the end of the hour, Sarah invited Sally to stay and meet for another hour.
Sarah left the room, called her family, and told them not to wait for her to
eat dinner. When she returned, she told Sally they could spend the next hour
saying goodbye and figuring out a game plan to support her. Sarah did her
best to develop an emotional bond with Sally as she opened up and spoke
honestly about her depression and her worry of disappointing her family.
Sally cried and Sarah's eyes, too, began to well up with tears. For the next
hour, the two became a therapy couple. Sarah tried her best to understand,
and the two developed a closeness. In the final minutes, Sarah told her what
to ask for in a therapist if she wanted her type of therapy. "Ask for someone who follows your lead, mostly listens, and strives to take an empathic
approach," Sarah said. Sally told her that she felt better. Sarah clicked off the
sound machine, walked to her car in darkness, and drove home. Glancing
back, she noticed a glowing farmhouse window.

Discussion

Science is a disciplined exploration. It requires investigating objective and
subjective material. For a treatment to be considered a member of the family
of evidence-based therapies, it requires incorporating the objective (replicable research), the clinician's judgement, and the subjective preferences of
the patient. It is essential that the patient's preferences be accounted for and
considered.

In the above clinical-based intervention, it became clear that Sally
wanted an empathic-based treatment, rather than a manualized, theory-first
approach. Sarah wondered, when Sally asked how Sarah would respond to
a suicidal patient, if Sally needed to idealize the therapist's confidence. Perhaps Sally needed to look up to Sarah's ability to help her. Like when a
home is on fire, the occupants need to idealize the firefighter's ability to
put out the blaze to save them. Sarah's comment about how she approached
an adult's suffering was an attempt to welcome a "curative fantasy." That is,
it was Sarah's attempt to join with Sally's hope that her life could improve.
Sarah hoped that Sally could borrow her strength and if she was confident,
maybe Sally could be, too.

Sarah answered Sally's question. Answering questions nearly always deep-
ens the therapy (Brandchaft, Doctors, & Sorter, 2010). Sally truly wanted
to know how a Healing the Self approach might differ from her current
therapy. Interestingly, because Sarah's approach was different, it could have

invited Sally to distance herself from her individual therapist. However, because Sally was soon to be discharged, it appeared worth the risk. Sarah explaining how she worked was an effort to empower Sally to find a therapist that could accommodate Sally's preferences.

Because Sally clearly sought an empathic treatment approach, Sarah was also trying to communicate that she would stand side-by-side with Sally. This was the first step in becoming emotionally very close (Geist, 2019). By allowing herself to feel with Sally, Sarah communicated that Sally's emotions weren't destructive and could be contained, understood, and felt; they could be a conduit for closeness with another person.

The therapist's feelings have the power to help or hurt the therapy. The general rule is that the therapist can, of course, be genuine, but not at the patient's expense. This requires a high degree of self-awareness and the ability to prioritize the patient's experience (Teicholz, 2014). When Sarah silently wept with Sally, it showed that she cared and meant that she understood Sally's suffering. This shared emotional experience also helped create a sense of belonging. Although not a full therapy case, for that brief two hours, Sally felt known and connected to another.

Sarah communicated that Sally was worth knowing. In this sense, Sarah's empathic stance enabled Sally to experience a sense of belonging. Belonging is critical because a thwarted sense of belonging is a primary risk factor of suicide (Joiner, 2005). Sally belonged to Sarah, and the two of them had a connection.

Sally longed for a therapist that was engaged empathically with her. She tolerated the outdoor activities, but these activities didn't heighten her mood. Interestingly, research regarding the psychological effects of "thru" hiking the Appalachian Trail (AT) suggests that hiking can be immensely beneficial for AT hikers. AT thru-hikers report noteworthy psychological change, including a reduction in psychotic symptoms. This does not happen, however, because of the exercise, nature, or the camping element. Hikers attributed psychological change to a sense of community and belonging that occurs because of human relationships that exist on the AT (Ketterer, 2010).

The above vignette is not a full treatment case study. Although it is only a brief encounter, it indicates the importance of including the patient's perspective. South African neuroscientist Dr. Mark Solms reminds us that studying and working with people is different from other sciences because people talk. If you want to understand someone's neurological experience, ask them about it (Solms, 2015). Sally demonstrated that she wanted a therapy that spoke to her.

Learning Activities

Your subjective experience is a key part of evidence-based practice. Do you agree with any of the features of the Healing the Self model? Do you believe that it would pass the "Grandmother Test"? Would your grandmother or a reasonable grandmother you know find the model useful? In the spirit of testing the hypothesis, write a paragraph or two outlining your experience of the model as a whole. Be sure to include if you believe the model would or wouldn't be endorsed by your grandmother.

Application Activities

Think like a scientist. Consider adopting the Healing the Self model in your classroom. Perform a simple pre-post test study. List some of the behaviors your class is demonstrating. For instance, the class is fidgeting, not paying attention, and disruptive. Also include your subjective experience of the class. For instance, you may "click" better with some students than with others. Then attempt to use Healing the Self. After striving to be admirable, empathic, and create a sense of belonging with your students, did you notice a difference? If so, what did you notice? More importantly, if you didn't notice a change, what are your thoughts as to why? The important aspect of this exercise it to play with the idea of thinking scientifically.

References

APA Task Force. (2005). Evidence-based practice in psychology. *American Psychologist, 61*(4), 271–285.

Ardito, R. B., & Rabellino, D. (2011). Therapeutic alliance and outcome psychotherapy: Historical excursus, measurements, and prospective for research. *Frontiers in Psychology, 2,* 270–275. doi:10.3389/fpsyq2011.00270

Bandcraft, B., Doctors, S., & Sorter, D. (2010). *Toward an emancipatory psychoanalysis.* New York, NY: Routledge.

di Pellegrino, G., Fadiga, L., Fogassi, L., Gallese, V., & Rizzolatti, G. (1992). Understanding motor events: A neurophysiological study. *Experimental Brain Research, 91*(1), 176–180.

Eisenberger, N. I. (2012). The neural bases of social pain: Evidence for shared representations with physical pain. *Psychosomatic Medicine, 74*(2), 126–135. doi:10.1097/PSY.0b013e3182464dd1

Eisenberger, N. I., & Lieberman, M. D. (2004). Why rejection hurts: A common neural alarm system for physical and social pain. *Trends in Cognitive Sciences, 8*(7), 294–300. doi:10.1016/j.tics.2004.05.010

Geist, R. (2019). Discussion of James Herzog's case: Dolph and Gus. *Psychoanalysis, Self and Context, 13*(1), 73–79.

Joiner, T. E. (2005). *Why people die by suicide.* Cambridge, MA: Harvard University Press.

Kanwisher, N., Stanley, D., & Harris, A. (1999). The fusiform face area is selective for faces not animals. *Neuroreport, 10*(1), 183–187.

Ketterer, W. (2010). *Psychological change among Appalachian trail thru-hikers: An interpretive phenomenological analysis* (Doctoral Dissertation), Ann Arbor, MI, UMI Dissertation Publishing.

Norcross, J. C., & Wampold, B. E. (2011). Evidence-based therapy relationships: Research conclusions and clinical practices. *Psychotherapy, 48*(1), 98–102.

Ornstein, A. (2017). Special challenges facing child therapists. *Psychanalysis, Self and Context, 12,* 346–355.

Rosenzweig, S. (1936). Some implicit common factors in diverse methods of psychotherapy: "At last" the Dodo said, "Everybody has won and all must have prizes". *American Journal of Orthopsychiatry, 6,* 412–415.

Sackett, D. L., Rosenberg, J. A., Gray, R., Haynes, B., & Richardson, W. S. (1996). Evidence-based medicine: What it is and what it isn't. *British Journal of Medicine, 312,* 71–72.

Saxe, R., & Kanwisher, N. (2003). People thinking about thinking people: The role of the temporo-parietal junction in "theory of mind". *NeuroImage, 19*(4), 1835–1842. doi:10.1016/S1053-8119(03)00230-1

Seung, S. (2012). *Connectum: How the brain's wiring makes us who we are.* Boston, MA: Houghton Mifflin Harcourt.

Shedler, J. (2010). The efficacy of psychodynamic psychotherapy. *American Psychologist, 65,* 98–109. doi:10.1037/a0018378.

Solms, M. (2015). *The feeling brain: Selected papers on neuropsychoanalysis.* London, England: Karnac Books.

Spreng, R.N., & Grady, C.L. (2010). Patterns of brain activity supporting autobiographical memory, prospection, and theory of the mind and their relationship to the default mode network. *Journal of Cogitative Neuroscience, 22*(6), 112–123.

Teicholz, J.G. (2014). Treating Trauma: The Analyst's Own Affect Regulation and Expression. *Psychoanalytic Inquiry, 34*(4), 364–379.

Wampold, B. (2015). How important are the common factors in psychotherapy? An update. *World Psychiatry, 14*(3), 270–277.

Yalom, I. D., & Leszcz, M. (2005). *The theory and practice of group psychotherapy.* New York, NY: Basic Books.

9   Healing the Self in the School

As has been emphasized in previous chapters, the Healing the Self model was developed from evidence-based psychotherapy approaches that have been demonstrated to reduce anger, anxiety, and other emotional turmoil. The foundation of this model is the assumption that relationships need not be traditionally "therapeutic" to help children, meaning that teachers, counselors, mentors, principals, teacher assistants, and others can and do provide children with the necessary ingredients to build and maintain self-esteem through their school-based relationships. Healing the Self provides a framework for teachers and others to apply evidence-based, psychotherapeutically derived skills and concepts in the classroom.

However, using therapeutic concepts in an educational setting demands special considerations. This chapter outlines some of the differences between application in schools and application in a therapeutic setting. Although there are many similarities between schools and therapy clinics, in terms of working with children to build self-esteem and create meaningful relationships, there is one primary difference and that is the way in which trust is established. This chapter outlines how schools can attempt to build trust with families, then explores how to bridge the home-school divide.

Therapy settings and therapeutic work are uniquely designed to create trust above all other virtues. Trust is vital, for without it growth is impossible. Without trust and confidence, therapy is a phony shell game.

Typically in psychotherapy, one person suffers and seeks assistance from another person. The suffering person or patient wants to feel better and pays the therapist to help him or her do so, which requires an agreement. The suffering person agrees to pay the therapist and the therapist agrees to help the patient. In essence, the patient invites the therapist into his or her life and wants their help. In this context, there is the implied understanding that either party is free to leave if the patient's difficulties don't improve. The patient can find another therapist, and the therapist, although this is often advised against, can refer the patient to another provider or a different form of treatment. Typically, trust is developed because both people enter the relationship willingly and are free to leave if they want to. This mutuality and liberty helps to engender confidence in their relationship. The ability of both parties to exit strengthens the contract (Hirschman, 1970). In the clinical setting these agreements create a form of teamwork sometimes called the "therapeutic alliance." In an alliance there is a sense of working together and trust is then developed (Safran & Muran, 2000).

The nature of the agreement between a teaching institution and a student, however, is different. In public schools and special education, most students do not enter a relationship with their teacher voluntarily. Neither they nor their families can hand-pick the school they wish to attend or the teacher they want to instruct them. Parents are generally not free to shop around looking for the best fit between their child and a teacher, nor are all families able to remove their child from the school if they are unhappy. Not only must the student stay but so, too, must the teacher. Public school teachers educate all the students who come to them, regardless of ability, need, or fit with their particular teaching style. Further complicating matters, if anyone in the equation (teacher, parent, or student) makes a blunder, it's often difficult or impossible to transfer the student and/or leave. In schools, a teacher, school counselor, principal, or other faculty may have to face the student the next day if there was a mistake. In fact, in some communities, the same teacher may work with the student again, plus his or her siblings and possibly their children, years later!

Thus, unlike therapy, where two people choose to work together, in schools there may not be a mutually agreed upon relationship. In this way, a public school can sometimes be likened to an arranged marriage. Because the relationship has not been freely chosen between both parties, a symbiotic alliance is especially difficult to create in schools. A sense of teamwork or alliance may not naturally exist and thus trust is harder to establish than in a therapy setting.

When problems arise, difficult student behaviors can get very complicated for teachers and other school staff because they are not typically invited into the student's life or his family's life. Most families do not send their children to school hoping their child's teacher or principal will be calling them to discuss their child's difficulties at school. School is not designed to be a place of therapy. Yet, in order to teach students, schools are required to address children's social and emotional needs. Thus, if the task of educating students, especially those with anger and/or aggressive behaviors, is going to be accomplished, trust is vitally important—as important in schools as it is in therapy.

To help engender this trust (and therefore be able to implement the Healing the Self concepts in schools) educators can borrow the following three specific time-tested concepts from therapists to aid them in implementation:

1. Be an invited guest.
2. Understand emotional difficulties as adaptive in context.
3. Cultivate pride.

By Invitation Only

The first way teachers, principals, and other personnel can help build trust in the school setting is to consider the concept of becoming an invited guest. The idea of the "invited guest" means that processing or otherwise discussing something with a child should only be done *after* the teacher or principal or others *ask permission*. That is, by asking permission to discuss or process with a child about something he or she did, the school is allowing the child, family, or guardian a way out. By granting permission to "leave," faculty is indirectly encouraging trust. Students can't leave school and parents often find ways to disengage from schools they don't want to deal with. Thus, both students and parents will find ways to "check-out"—to stop participating in school in a collaborative way. To help them engage again and to build trust, educators must ask permission to be a part of the student's life—to help the family feel as if they have choices about how things will proceed and to allow them the chance to withdraw emotionally if necessary.

The following statements are examples of asking permission and attempting to be an invited guest in the life of a student and his or her family:

- May I discuss this with you?
- Would you be willing to meet with us/me?
- Is it okay if we talk about this now?

In a therapy agreement, the therapist is invited to help. But school personnel, although in a position to help students a great deal, aren't often invited by the child or the parents to insert themselves into a student's personal problems. That's why if during a discussion a student no longer wants to talk, the talking should stop. Everyone's thoughts, feelings, and wishes are private. Although behaviors are often public and can be seen, everyone's emotional world is their own. Because teachers and students cannot easily leave each other, the concept of the invited guest creates a safety check that enables students a way out of a situation they may interpret as threatening. Many teachers can create a way out as well by asking someone else to talk to the student.

Think of the invited guest concept like an invitation for tea. The student or their parents may at first want a cup of tea, so to speak, but then later decide that they don't. Of course, at a tea party if a person doesn't like their tea they can stop drinking it at any time. The same goes with discussions at school about behavior, emotional problems, family issues, and so forth. Be respectful of a student's right to change their mind about having that "cup of tea." Everyone benefits from teaching children that "No" means "No." Discussing feelings requires consent. This isn't to say or otherwise imply that students shouldn't receive consequences for their misbehavior. Of course, kids need discipline, and if a student misbehaves a reasonable consequence that fits is necessary. It is easy for counseling or processing of the event to serve as a consequence in and of itself. Of course, although unintended, this may weaponize the counseling in the child's mind. If the child believes the counseling is the consequence, it may unintentionally have little effect in helping the child grow. With that said, the invited guest concept is one of the best ways to build confidence in schools and serves as a reminder that trust is enhanced when people have the ability to leave.

Understand Problems as Adaptive

In therapy, the patient and therapist have an agreement that the work's focus is on alleviating the patient's suffering. They also usually agree upon the nature of the problem for which the patient is seeking help, i.e., the patient entered therapy for help with depression or anger, for example. Sometimes there isn't agreement—it's just that the patient wants to change in some way. Many times, however, the initial problem people seek treatment for isn't the actual problem holding them back (McWilliams, 2004).

In school, there isn't necessarily an agreement about the nature of the problem. Is it the student's misbehavior, the family's engagement, or the school's approach? Moreover, parents, teachers, and students may not see the same problem. It may be very difficult for everyone to agree that a student has a particular difficulty or even the nature of that difficulty. As a result, all involved can be playing the "blame game," where accountability is punted through cross-criticism. Of course, the willingness to recognize human shortcomings (which we all have) requires durable self-esteem and there are important reasons why sometimes teachers, families, and students don't "see" the problem.

One way that schools can avoid or reduce the blame game is to consider the student's difficulties as adaptive in another context. This means that if the problem is seen from the child's perspective, the sometimes-diagnosable disorder can actually be a reasonable attempt by the child to try to hold himself or herself together. In this way emotional problems can be considered a child's effort to protect fragile self-esteem, as well as their best attempt at relating to others. For instance, let's say a student we'll call Bob, disobeys simple, straightforward instructions and is so oppositional and defiant that he meets DSM-5 diagnostic criteria for Oppositional Defiant Disorder (ODD). On the one hand, Bob is very defiant, but perhaps understood in context his defiance is actually adaptive to his situation. Perhaps Bob comes from a home where in his mind following the adult's instructions would be a huge mistake. Maybe Bob has witnessed adults behaving irresponsibly or engaging in unsafe activities. The problem then changes from being oppositional behavior to being seen as Bob needing to be adaptive to his particular circumstance, given the context at home. Moreover, perhaps his defiance is his attempt to tell the adult world that he, too, wants to be an adult and thus his defiance is an ill-fated attempt to join the grown-up world. Now the school may address the problematic behaviors from a new platform of understanding. In this sense, nearly all emotional difficulties or pathology can be considered adaptive in some way.

For another example let's take a look at Sarah, who clearly appears to be depressed at school. Her lack of energy, while seeming to be a straight-forward case of depression, could be very adaptive—she could be using the sadness (her lack of energy) to draw people to her and/or protect her from engaging in self-harming behaviors. In this way perhaps her low energy protects her. Likewise, she could learn to distract herself from her emotional pain by focusing on school work. Self-loathing could fuel academic success.

Thinking of problems in terms of context avoids the necessity of an agree-ment to the problem by the school and the student's family. That is, rather than agreeing that a student, Billy, has ADHD, the school must merely do its best to enable Billy to focus at school. The difference may appear subtle, but in practice, when parties do not have to agree to the nature of the problem it may prevent power struggles and reduce ill will between everyone. This helps build trust.

Sometimes it seems clear that the child's problem can be easily identified as actually the parent(s)' problem. Often teachers have sat in meetings and thought, "if only the family could straighten out, sober up, be nice, stop get-ting arrested . . . then little Johnny's difficulties would vanish." This is danger-ous ground and rarely helpful because children experience that their parents are actually part of themselves. Thinking the family is bad is like labeling a part of the child as bad—the two are intertwined within a child's world (Ornstein, 2017). Experience suggests that children can sense when faculty or therapists don't like and accept their family and it blocks trust. Trust among educators, families, and students is best cultivated when such thinking is avoided.

Cultivate Pride

Pride is a fundamental human need. Just as children require adults to validate them, adults also need to feel proud of the child's accomplishments as well as their own parenting. Adults working with challenging children must recog-nize the family's need to feel proud in order to invest and connect with both the child's emotional growth and the school or therapist (Ornstein, 2017).

There are three ways to increase a sense of pride. The first is simple. Schools may greatly benefit from showcasing student work, achievements, or other aspects of the student's strengths. Show the parents, community, and others what the child can do. Yes, little Bobby may have difficulties with anger, but before we discuss our plan, let's listen to him read, or admire his artwork and/or building projects. Let's watch him perform well in athletics, or see him in positive social interactions.

A second way to increase pride is to be aware of parental guilt and dis-appointment. Clinical experience suggests that sometimes if educators are simply aware of the student's and their parents' sensitivity to shame, this can be enough. Working with or rearing a symptomatic child is exhausting. The adults (parents, teachers, therapist, pediatrician, faith-based leader) can easily feel guilty. Guilt distracts adults from caring for children (Olden, 1953). Adults often try to avoid the guilt by either retaliating against the child or by over-indulging them. It's easy for adults working with children to inadvertently increase the sense of parental guilt and further distance the family and child from a sense of pride.

One way adults try to avoid feeling guilty about a symptomatic child is by directly or indirectly demonstrating that they are perfect (Ornstein, 2017). No one is perfect and although idealization is necessary for children to grow, attempting to convince everyone of our infallibility is rarely helpful. Although counterintuitive, when a teacher or school strives to be perfect it can be an indication of adult guilt and shame, which impedes the ability to be proud.

At times, children can attempt to shame their parents. They can use their teachers to try to hurt their mom and dad. For example, when Cindy says, "Mom, Mr. Smith would never raise his voice at me," it can be an attempt to hurt the parents. It is important that teachers and families keep the Healing the Self concepts in their mind and consider how their attempts at implementing idealization, empathy, and belonging can be weaponized to inflict parental shame.

A third approach to increasing pride relies on empathy. When school personnel are able to feel, think, sense, and otherwise understand the parents' perspective it can open doors to relatedness. That is, when someone understands another and doesn't reject them it welcomes them to lower their guard. Child therapists attempt to do this by validating parents' difficulties with a symptomatic child (Ornstein, 2015). For instance, a therapist may empathize with a parent by saying such things as:

- It is difficult to keep Billy organized, isn't it?
- Tough transition?
- Another grumpy morning?

Just as empathy is important for the child, it is important for the parents of the child. Parents need understanding and acceptance in the sometimes exhausting efforts to teach and train their children. School personnel who show families empathy are helping ensure that a sense of pride is being cultivated in both children and their parents. But sometimes, despite everyone's intentions, home-school divides emerge.

Bridging a Possible Home-School Divide

Every family wants the best for their children, and all schools want to be their best, too, but not everyone agrees about what exactly defines "the best" or how to provide it. Unfortunately, even when schools strive to develop trust with families, and families support their children's school, seemingly impossible divisions can develop. In this section, we examine additional considerations for families and schools to ponder in an effort to better understand the complexities of the school-family relationship. Both parents and schools can have powerful reactions to one another, and these reactions can be understood empathically by outlining some of the possible crossroads at which schools and families may find themselves at odds. By examining these junctures, we can build a foundation of understanding to allow schools and families to work together to effectively and cooperatively support their children.

Parents

For some people, schools are temples of knowledge, wisdom, and the imagination. Schools strive to be fundamentally good places that nurture the intellect. Schools aim to confirm that you're smart, valued, and capable. For others, schools can be a place of disappointment, frustration, and shame. Families may wish to protect their children from the disappointments, criticisms, and sometimes harsh judgments that schools dish out. Some parents oppose schools because of their own negative history with them. Their dislike for schools serves to protect them and their children from new or ongoing terrible disappointments.

Schools inherently measure academic achievement, and many parents and children experience schools as measuring not only the student's mastery of skills, but the child themselves. As many schools adopt the philosophy of teaching the whole child, the stakes can feel even higher. Now, schools judge not only how well the student reads, but his or her study skills, ability to socialize, and perhaps even their character. An unintended consequence is that families can feel judged and criticized when schools deem their child's character lacking, or needing improvement, in some way.

Most parents want their child to succeed in school, and parents can be disheartened to learn that their child has difficulties. Schools are often the first to inform families that their son or daughter has trouble learning or socializing. This is because schools know the trajectory of typical learning, and they must provide families with honest appraisals of a child's abilities. When a student demonstrates difficulties, school can provide early intervention to overcome the hurdle. All this, however, can be very difficult for families to absorb because it destroys the family's fantasy that junior can be anything he wants to be. School can be the first place where a child doesn't make the grade or the team. Schools, sometimes, must report bad news, and families may have difficulty separating the news itself from the messenger.

For others, disliking schools provides a vitally important cohesive function. Some families feel broken, and opposing the school rallies everyone toward a common goal. "We all think so-and-so school is crummy. That's our collective opinion."

Schools

Conversely, teachers, counselors, principals, and others may find themselves terribly frustrated with families. Few occupations are as dependent on other people as teaching. When parents allow their child to stay up all night playing video games, it's the teacher who has to pay the next morning. No teacher likes having to call the Department of Child and Family Services (DCFS), but all teachers and adults who work with children are mandated to do so when they suspect abuse or neglect in the home. When parents don't parent their children, teaching the kids can seem an insurmountable obstacle. Teachers can't ignore their students' social and emotional needs—emotional needs that are created by parent behaviors. For instance, imagine how difficult it is for a teacher to console a student whose parent was incarcerated. Further complicating matters, when one child has difficulty, it can sometimes disrupt the entire class or school.

When a family's attitude about school is negative, the teachers may struggle daily to balance their investment in their students against this negativity. When an angry parent yells at a teacher, the teacher may withdraw his or her investment in the child's success to protect themselves from caring too much and being hurt. The worst-case scenario is when parents tell their children that they don't have to listen to or follow the teacher's directions; this shatters the teacher-parent alliance. When this happens, it prevents healthy idealization and halts academic progress. If the parents communicate that the teacher need not be listened to, then when the student listens to the teacher, he or she is effectively disobeying the parent.

It can be very difficult for any teacher to tell students or parents bad news. Few teachers want to tell parents that their child is struggling. Moreover, some parents haven't had their relational needs met, so they retaliate against the teacher. "It's your fault that he can't read," disappointed parents have said. This sentiment holds true at the university level as well. An organic chemistry professor once disclosed that his class weeded out potential medical school applicants. He said the hardest part of his job was giving honest grades to hard-working students. Schools have to tell people bad news, and bad news is often difficult to accept.

Further complicating the family-school dynamic is that children can strive to have their relationship needs met in ways that close off opportunities. In these instances, children may unintentionally pit idealization needs against belonging needs.

Idealization Versus Belonging

Empathic attunement, idealization, and a sense of belonging are psychological needs as real as the human need for food, water, and oxygen. Like physical needs, they must be met, and depending on the relational environment available to him or her, they are met either in a pro-social context or in a maladaptive way (Rowe & Rowe Clay, 1991). Hopefully the home and school can meet these psychological requirements in concert, resulting in the child developing enduring self-esteem. However, because these relational needs are vital, children urgently try to meet them. This process can echo the old lifeguard warning: "Approach a drowning swimmer cautiously, because their efforts to stay afloat may drown you." Because children require interpersonal relationships that provide for these psychological needs, a child may inadvertently "drown" one need provider for the sake of another.

Children require adults that they can idealize, but they also require a sense of belonging. These two needs can unintentionally oppose each other. For instance, a student may wish to idealize his or her teacher, but in the home, if education isn't valued, then idealizing the teacher jeopardizes their sense of belonging within the family. It can become school versus home. Parents can sometimes experience the student's admiration for the teacher as an indication of their own low self-worth. It can be painful for some parents to hear how great and successful their child's teacher is when the parent feels he or she hasn't measured up. Moreover, if education isn't valued in the family, then pursuing an education can disrupt both the student and their family's identity. How education can de-idealize parents and disrupt a family's sense of belonging is most readily observable when discussing higher education.

An education can serve to de-idealize parents. In some families, if the child looks up to the teacher it means that he or she no longer idealizes a parent. How many times have we heard that when a college freshman returns home for Thanksgiving, they quickly tell their family that they learned how "wrong" they are? College taught them that their parents are outdated or don't know much. Their need to idealize the college experience costs them the idealization of their now perhaps financially drained parents.

Education can also strain family ties. For instance, a high school senior was accepted into a prestigious military college. Rather than being happy for his son, his father was disappointed that his son didn't want to enlist first. His father enlisted and didn't think highly of officers. The young man was tormented rather than overjoyed by his acceptance and impending decision. The son's education threatened his psychological place in the home, as well as his identity as a loyal son.

Going away to college and choosing a different career path than your parent are examples of the complexities of relational needs and how meeting one need can interfere with meeting the other. The same can happen when a particular need is met through a certain relationship, which can then prevent other relationships from meeting those same needs.

There are no easy answers to these dilemmas, but understanding that both parents and teachers have legitimate frustrations can be useful in bridging the relational divide. Experience shows that when schools can understand the parents' perspective, and the parents can empathize with the school, a bridge can be built between them.

Healing the Self in Schools Case Study: Erin's Voice

Erin entered a new school at the start of her fourth-grade year. She had moved to town with her mother from another nearby state and her parents were not together, though she saw her father most weekends. Erin had struggled at her previous school and her mother removed her because the school wanted to place Erin in an out of district alternative school. Her mother enrolled her in the new school because it offered a smaller class and weekly access to a therapist.

During her early weeks in the new school, Erin rarely spoke. In fact, multiple times a day she fled the classroom and hid. The staff worried as they searched the school for her. They found her hiding in different places. Her mother reported to the school that Erin had done this a lot in her previous school. She said Erin also became angry. She slapped, punched, and kicked teachers whenever she felt trapped by them. Her mother warned the school that Erin was very, very anxious.

School work was easy for Erin, but she hadn't been able to tolerate spending time in the larger classroom at her former school and barely tolerated the smaller classroom at her new school. Erin's teacher and others went to great lengths to engage and connect with her. Over time she stopped running out of class. She was able to remain in the classroom even when she was angry or anxious. Although these were important gains, she still rarely spoke. Eventually Erin became comfortable with her teacher, Amy. In private, Erin spoke single words (yes, no, and maybe) to Amy, but she never talked to peers.

The first time she met the school's therapist, Paul, Erin didn't say a word. She came to the school office willingly, sat down with an expressionless face, and played with putty on Paul's table. One day she spotted some gel pens on Paul's desk and gestured toward them. Paul wordlessly handed her paper and some of the pens. In that instance, Paul felt Erin's worry with her as they both sat silently. Paul broke the silence and asked her if she was okay sitting with him. Erin answered him with a cold stare. This routine repeated itself during the first two sessions—they sat in silence while Erin drew or fidgeted with putty.

In their third meeting, Paul decided not to speak first. Paul wondered if maybe Erin thought adults were too weak to hold her terrible feelings. Maybe by being silent he would show Erin he was tough enough to be there for her. Of course, he thought if Erin looked upset he would talk to her. When Erin sat down, Paul took out a blank piece of white paper and drew swirling, looping lines with a pencil all over the paper. This created an abstract design with small and large spaces of various shapes. He then took a purple gel pen and started to color in one of the spaces. Erin watched him intently. After a few moments, Paul looked up and offered the pens to Erin. She took an orange pen and started to color in another space on the paper. They colored silently until all the spaces were filled in. The scribbles became a beautiful abstract mosaic of colors. Paul offered it to Erin, who accepted it in silence and happily returned to the classroom.

At their next meeting, as they entered the office, Erin asked, "Can we do that again? Will you draw the scribbles on the paper so we can color them in?" Paul was shocked. Erin had spoken! Paul silently celebrated then answered, "Of course."

As Erin sat down in her same spot she asked questions about color selections for their design, then disclosed her interests. During this session Erin finally opened up. She spoke freely about her likes and dislikes, worries and fears. Erin never disclosed the exact reason for her fury and fear of speaking, but only that she thought her feelings were simply too powerful to tell people and if she told the world how angry she was, everyone would reject her.

Over time, Paul introduced the idea of a "strong voice." He believed that Erin had a strong voice inside her that she had forgotten to use. They agreed that Erin would practice using her "strong voice" in their weekly meetings. Then, when Erin was ready, maybe she could use it in the classroom. They created and colored a squiggle drawing that had the words, "Use your strong voice!" in the center. Some days later, Paul noticed that Amy had laminated all their drawings and Erin had hung them near her desk.

Erin slowly became more engaged in her academics and Paul. Her teachers were careful to take notice of her strong intellect. Eventually, she did speak up in class. "Buzz off, you jerks," was one of the first things she said to a group of boys who had presumably been harassing her. Erin had found her strong voice!

Erin excelled at learning but feelings of worry and anger imprisoned her. She worried that others couldn't hear her anger, so she chose not to talk. In order for any form of therapy to work, the first step is to build trust. Paul was able to build this trust by being an invited guest, cultivating feelings of pride in Erin, and understanding her mutism as Erin's attempt at adapting to and dealing with her fears and circumstances. Erin required that Paul be very thoughtful and build trust before he could attempt to apply the Healing the Self method.

Discussion

Many school therapists may have approached Erin's difficulties by designing a reinforcement plan that rewarded Erin whenever she talked. Paul, however, took a different approach when he chose to use the Healing the Self model. He believed that trying to establish a strong interpersonal connection with Erin through empathy and acceptance could provide her confidence and security. Rather than trying to force Erin to talk about her feelings and worries, Paul followed her lead and her interests. By sitting with her quietly and waiting for her to talk he was attempting to be an invited guest and demonstrate, through his restraint, that he could be trusted. At the same time, being an invited guest also helped Erin admire Paul. Following her nonverbal cues, he drew with her and they connected through art. Paul demonstrated that he was worthy of her confidence when he played her game of silence and hoped this showed his resolve to follow her lead. This approach helped Erin admire Paul as an adult who was not trying to force her to be something she wasn't. She developed a sense of trust.

Paul never saw Erin's mutism as a symptom that had to be resolved. Rather, he wondered what role it played in her life and how it provided a clue regarding how to approach her. Although Paul eventually learned that Erin was quiet to protect others from her dangerous feelings, he also learned that her silence was her best attempt at asking an adult to see things her way—for the adult to contain his or her urge to do something, in this case to speak, just as she had to contain nasty feelings brooding deep inside her.

Paul helped Erin take pride in her art. Moreover, she had a special drawing language and ritual that enabled her to feel like she belonged and that her way of engaging Paul was meaningful. Through art and Paul's patience, Erin found her voice. By the end of the school year, Erin talked, joked, played, and laughed with the many friends she had made. She no longer fled the classroom and instead shared when she felt scared.

In conclusion, therapy and educational settings are different. Therapists have different roles than teachers and are charged with very different tasks. The Healing the Self model strives to create the therapeutic relationship of trust in the classroom by encouraging educators to be invited guests in their students' emotional worlds and by considering the adaptive context of the students' difficulties. By avoiding formal diagnosis, the model also bypasses some of the hurdles associated with therapy-based approaches in schools. Pride is important, and when adults working with children stay conscious of the need of parents to take pride in their student's accomplishments, it enables families to better connect with schools.

References

Hirschman, A. (1970). *Exit, voice, and loyalty: Response to declines in organizations, in firms, and states.* Cambridge, MA: Harvard University Press.

McWilliams, N. (2004). *Psychoanalytic psychotherapy: A practitioner's guide.* New York, NY: Guilford Press.

Olden, C. (1953). On adult empathy with children. *Psychoanalytic Study of the Child, 8,* 111–126.

Ornstein, A. (2015). Why Kohut's ideas will endure: The contributions of self psychology to the treatment of children and to the practice of psychotherapy. *International Journal of Psychoanalytic Self Psychology, 10*(2), 128–141.

Ornstein, A. (2017). Special challenges facing child therapists. *Psychoanalysis, Self and Context, 12,* 346–355.

Rowe, C. E., & Rowe Clay, D. (1991). *Empathic attunement: The "technique" of psychoanalytic self psychology.* New York, NY: Jason Aronson.

Safran, J. D., & Muran, C. J. (2000). *Negotiating the therapeutic alliance: A relational treatment guide.* New York, NY: Guilford Press.

Winnicott, D. W. (1976). *The child, the family, and the outside world.* New York, NY: Penguin Books.

10 Healing the Self in the Home

Children develop self-esteem through relationships. The most important relationship for any child, whether positive or negative, is with their parents and family. For many children their positive sense of self develops seamlessly in the home. The child admires their parents, who strive to understand him or her, and a strong sense of belonging and well-being naturally occurs. Sometimes, for any number of reasons, this process doesn't unfold naturally. When this process encounters obstacles, there are several concepts parents can keep in mind to assist them in caring for their children.

This section begins by encouraging parents to believe in themselves, then outlines unique aspects of applying Healing the Self in the home and how parents can implement these ideas with their families. It then discusses when an expert may, in fact, be needed, and concludes with a case study. In doing so, it attempts to tread carefully in the sacred space of the family living room.

Trust Yourself

Trust yourself as a parent. Remember the old counseling adage, "Use science when working with other people's children, rely on your own intuition and traditions first when rearing your own." Today, many parents are nervous to trust their instincts when parenting. The internet and other media are filled with "how to" videos on everything, especially parenting advice. There is no doubt that parenting advice and information helps many parents. However, parents often over focus on the advice of experts, ignoring their own intuition while raising their own children.

Perhaps surprisingly, expert advice can sometimes harm families and the creation of reliable, healthy family bonds (Sherwood & Cohen, 1994). In order for children to develop real, durable self-esteem, they need to connect with parents on a deep and genuine level. This requires the parent to be authentically present, engaged, and real. When parents rely too much on parenting books, classes, and YouTube videos for advice, they may be disregarding their own intuitions and the other things they know to be true and right for their child. Consequently, a danger emerges that the parenting technique itself interferes with closeness developing between parent and child. Children cannot connect to techniques or parenting systems; they need real adults who are present with them and have their own strong personalities and identities that a child can admire. In order for kids to develop self-esteem, they need adults to show up and be real. Overreliance on "experts" can interfere with parents being their true selves with their children.

Rearing children is as human an activity as eating or sleeping. Although not simple or easy, parenting is a natural process. It is something we learn to do from our own families. And, even when the families of origin did not have ideal parenting role models, almost all parents have a sense about how to parent and how they *want* their children to grow and develop. Not only can relying on experts interfere with parents being authentically present with their children (by following scripts and prescribed "parenting techniques"), it can also inadvertently reinforce parents' sense that they are not up for the job. More specifically, expert advice may inadvertently communicate that a family's traditions, rituals, faith-based practices, and accumulated generational knowledge is wrong or insufficient. The very stuff that can be idealized by children and foster belonging in families can be perceived as bad or wrong if it is at odds with the experts.

Relying on experts must be done cautiously, as it can disempower the very adults it's aiming to assist. Ironically, if the advice works, it could convince the parents their intuitive practices weren't good enough, and that the parents were deficient in their parenting. Although on the surface expert advice may seem helpful, it can also disempower parents and diminish the child's ability to admire the powerful, admirable adult. Similarly, if the advice or strategy fails, it may mean the expert was a charlatan, the theory was phony, or worse, the child is hopeless. For these reasons and others, parents are urged to be careful when seeking advice on childrearing. Likewise, we "experts" enter the home carefully for fear of causing more harm than good.

Healing at Home

There are features of this model that can be applied by parents. Parents, of course, are different from teachers, therapists, and others who care for children because of their emotional closeness to the child. There is no bond greater than the one between a parent and their child. When addressing children's and parents' self-esteem, the parent-child dyad is inseparable (Winnicott, 1965); whether biological or not, the child is psychologically part of the parent and vice versa (Ornstein, 1981).

Idealization Through Limit Setting

From infancy, children grow to idealize their parents. This complex, evolving, integral process enables developing a sense of self as capable, worthy, and powerful. While idealization happens naturally during infancy and toddlerhood, there are concepts that parents can bear in mind that may be of service to them as their children mature through these developmental stages.

Unlike teachers or therapists, parents usually aren't formally trained. Parenting doesn't come from a textbook or college class; it comes from the heart. Family life can be messy and busy. Parents can't structure their lives like a classroom, and parents can't use preplanned "scripts" for responding to all of their children's needs.

Parenting requires limit setting and boundaries. Limit setting is vital for healthy development, but parents may not realize that limit setting contributes to children admiring and idealizing them. Despite being necessary, many parents struggle with saying "No" to their children, and children are masters at getting to "Yes." When very young, a child may cry and carry on at bed time until mom or dad picks them up, satisfying their need for closeness and soothing. Eventually, however, the parent knows to set the limit that it's time for bed in order for the child (and parent, also) to meet their need for sleep. In this way, limit setting ensures that a child's physical, emotional, behavioral, and social needs are met. Through limit setting, children develop healthy admiration of their strong parent.

Setting limits contributes to children looking up to, admiring, and idealizing their parents. But why? Children who struggle with emotional regulation often experience the world around them as equally chaotic to their own feelings. These children require a predictable, constant, adult presence to help them develop the capacity to regulate their emotions. When parents provide structure and limits, it communicates that the world is safe and reliable and that although very important, the child's feelings do not run the world.

Limits permit the child to feel more calm, safe, and together, but also allows them to experience their parents as possessing astonishing power. The parent becomes the one who tames the child's inner turmoil that leaves the child feeling anxious, disappointed, out of control, and fragmented. Children admire this extraordinary power. As the child develops, he or she absorbs the idealized parent into their mind, enabling them to relinquish dependence on the external structure holding them to together and to have the self-esteem required to regulate their own emotions. This is not possible without adults providing limits which enable healthy idealization.

For many parents, limit setting can be challenging at times, but not an impossible problem. They internally recognize not to worry if their child gets mad at them or doesn't like them for the moment. There are also many parents who struggle with limit setting. Some parents had childhoods that may have been complicated by abuse, abandonment, or emotional restrictedness. Some of these parents may have learned as children that for families to function, negative feelings must be kept at bay and that negative feeling could destroy the ones they love (Doctors, 2017). Many people from families like these had to prioritize others and relinquish their own ambitions (Deutsch, 1942). Others learned that anger or other strong feelings lead to rejection or violence, making negative feelings intolerable, or even dangerous. As a consequence, parents from such backgrounds may not comfortably manage and tolerate their children's strong feelings, which can feel as scary as their own (Miller, 2008). Moreover, some parents come from families that prohibited strong emotions to such an extent that it impacted their ability to develop an individual identity (Sherwood & Cohen, 1994). Since limit setting often invokes strong feelings from the child, for these parents, limit setting can be a challenge.

Despite these challenges, parents can improve their ability to set limits. Limit setting requires tolerating the child's frustration and disappointment. It demands that the adult not be afraid of the child's feelings; in fact, as discussed below in the context of empathy, effective limit setting requires the parent holding the child's strong, negative feelings. This can be an unfamiliar task because many adults haven't been provided an emotional environment that allowed them to experience the full range of their *own* feelings. How can junior's negative feelings not feel threatening when parents were never permitted to access their own? To emotionally survive the negative feelings that limit setting provokes, parents require an atmosphere that encourages them to access the entirety of their emotional worlds including disappointment, sadness, frustrations, and even rage—the very feelings that may have been disallowed to them as children. When adults can access their unhappy feelings, it lessens their discomfort with a child's negative emotions.

Encouraging parents to consider what, if any, parts of themselves they have disavowed enables them to understand the important reasons why setting limits may be difficult. Setting limits requires adults to be able to feel all of their feelings. To do this, parents may benefit from utilizing their own emotional supports: family, friends, faith-based groups, and/or other communities, as well as considering their own personal psychotherapy. Personal psychotherapy provides an opportunity for people to access all their feelings without the risk of retaliation and/or abandonment. Therapy can not only support the adults' emotional needs, but it can also assist them in developing the capacity to set limits and hold limits with their children who depend on them.

Imperfect Empathy

Infants begin to learn self-regulation of their bodies and emotions through soothing and reflective responses from their parents when they are uncomfortable, excited, fearful, happy, or frustrated. This process is referred to as empathic attunement. It is the parent understanding what their child is experiencing and reflecting it back to them through their behavior, sounds, and words (Kohut, 1968). It is empathy and the beginnings of idealization when the child realizes in their own way, "Wow, this big person, who I admire, gets me!"

Empathy is unique for parents. Families share a similarity and connectedness that children can't match in their relationships at schools or clinics. In some families, the child was once biologically part of the parent, and there is an inherent bond and closeness between parent and child. Of course, not all families are comprised of biological children and parents. Most often, whether through nature or nurture, children are similar to their parents and this likeness lends itself readily to empathic understanding. The more similar you are to someone, the easier it is to be empathic (Kohut, 1971).

However, parents have needs, too, and the silent expectation is that both the child and the parent strive to meet each other's needs. Whereas a professional, be it teacher, counselor, or therapist, has his or her needs met financially, parents expect, to some degree, their daughter or son will validate their good parenting. Hopefully, the parent strives to parent and the child eagerly wishes to please his or her mom or dad. Think of the old adage, "He's a chip off the old block." Children want to make their parents proud, and parents want to see their parenting efforts affirmed by their child's successes. This is a critical aspect of parental empathy. On one hand, because children are like their parents, it's easier. On the other hand, stakes are much higher because there is the expectation that the child will meet his or her parents' emotional needs.

Just as limit setting requires a firm identity, empathy requires adults to bracket their own experience, thoughts, feelings, or identity and think, feel, and imagine their way into their child's experience. Although both limit setting and empathy are skills that can be learned, in general terms, some people are simply better at one than the other.

Perfect parenting is impossible, and maintaining an empathic stance with a child for prolonged periods of time is taxing. Whereas the teacher or counselor can attempt to take an empathic stance with a student or client for a set period of time, a constant empathic stance is impractical. Some theorists believe that even the best therapists can only partially maintain an empathic stance for moments of a psychotherapy session, and this can be enough to facilitate change. Therefore, the task for parents is to learn to be attentive to those times when empathic parenting is most needed by their child or children. In other words, effective parents do not need to be empathic *all the time*, but need to remain alert to those critical times when empathy fosters their child's growth and emotional development. Empathy can be tough, and we are all better at maintaining an empathic stance when our own empathic needs are met. This happens when we have others in our lives who routinely validate our experience and reinforce our interpersonal connection through empathic understanding.

Donald Winnicott coined the term the "good enough mother." The good enough mother or parent is the one that gets it right enough of the time with their children and who meets their child's emotional needs enough to foster a healthy sense of self in the child. Winnicott suggests that children actually benefit from parental failures (Winnicott, 1953). If these failures are modest, then they allow the child the opportunity to develop resiliency, which opens future opportunities and insulates them from later emotional difficulties in life. Parenting mistakes actually help kids.

Finally, parents need empathy from other parents and adults, too. Parenting is tough and working with a symptomatic child is challenging. Just as with teachers, counselors, and other professionals, parents should know when they are depleted. The old therapist wisdom may be useful. "Sometimes the empathy switch has to be turned off." Parents must have breaks from their responsibilities and have time with likeminded adults to maintain a healthy perspective on parenting.

Belonging and Acceptance

Acceptance and belonging are fundamental needs. Belonging differs at home when compared to a school or clinic. Children require a close, loving relationship with their parents and through emotional closeness, a sense of belonging grows. Just the concept of "family" creates in its members a sense of belonging. If you are a member of a family, you, by definition, belong to this unique group of people. Family is the cornerstone of belonging and emotional closeness.

Acceptance is key for children to feel like they are wanted and belong in their families. Sometimes parents accepting their children unconditionally can be tricky. Of course, parents want to accept and love their children for who they are, but it is also the parent's role to guide and teach their children effective ways of coping and navigating the world. On one hand, parents want their child to belong to them and their home, but on the other hand, some behaviors don't "belong" in the home.

Traditions, customs, faith-based practices, and other rituals enhance children's sense of belonging to the family. Children develop this sense by feeling cherished and wanted. Rituals can boost this process by providing a structure to belong to. For instance, in the child's mind the logic follows like this: "We are the Smiths. Smiths eat pizza and play cards together on Friday evenings." Friday's pizza party ritual assists in defining what it means to be a member of the Smith family. "Smiths are Friday night pizza-eaters and card players." Simply put, rituals assist in defining families, thus solidifying the family group that the child can belong to.

Moreover, many families experience an increased internal sense of belonging through community. Families can increase the child's sense that he or she is cherished, and thus cherish-able, by participating in any number of activities and groups that welcome children and their families. Faith-based groups, athletics, clubs, scouts, and countless other organizations can assist families in communicating a sense of belonging to their children. Just as rituals help in defining a family, community involvement can reinforce that sense that the child is wanted. For example, "We are Smiths, who on Friday's eat pizza and play cards, and we go to chapel. At chapel, we are wanted." In the child's mind the idea is, "I am a Smith, Smiths are wanted, I am wanted too." In this way, rituals help define a family, and community involvement helps families develop a sense of belonging.

Unfortunately, the children (and sometimes families) who need acceptance in groups the most often act in ways that cause the group to reject them. Children who struggle with anger and behave violently are often excluded from athletics, extracurricular activities, or play dates with peers. It can become a vicious cycle. Children suffering from low self-esteem often express anger and behave violently, and are subsequently shunned by their peers. This exclusion then reinforces his or her sense of isolation which further decreases self-esteem. There is no easy answer to solving this conundrum, but families being aware of these issues may assist them in better understanding their child's dilemma and thus provide an avenue for closeness.

Just as children can meet their belonging needs in maladaptive ways, so can families. Because the need to belong is so important, families can unknowingly meet that need in ways that unintentionally harm their children. One maladaptive way that families create a sense cohesion and closeness is by pitting themselves against other families and institutions. This is the "us vs. them" mentality. In this scenario, families reinforce often fragile or unstable family bonds by uniting in opposition against their child's school. This topic is discussed in detail in a following chapter. Kohut reminds us that it's easy to enjoy the warm feeling people get when they agree to be against another group of people (Elison, 1987). When parents forge a sense of belonging by being against others, particularly their children's school, it can have negative consequences.

When Therapy Is Required

Of course, sometimes families need help. When children suffer with low self-esteem, are overly angry, or behave violently, sometimes experts are needed. Clinical experience indicates that after being provided the above caveats, and when parents believe that their son or daughter needs outside help, they are usually right. When looking for a therapist, there are key steps to follow. A practical first step is to begin with your child's pediatrician and ask for help. This can be a difficult, but necessary, task. Your pediatrician can help you find a therapist. When looking for a therapist, it is important to remember that there are many, many different therapeutic approaches. The point of this section is not to burden parents with clinical responsibilities (those are the job of the therapist), but to provide them very basic understanding of some of the interventions that professionals can provide.

Family Therapy

Family therapy is when a clinician meets with the family to better understand the relational dynamics. It can serve to help put conflicts into words, which allows them to be understood, managed, and provide insights that encourages the healing process. Family therapy can be immensely helpful, but sometimes getting everyone together or recognizing that everyone needs to consider changing isn't possible. There are many different family therapy approaches. Like all approaches, sometimes families benefit and sometimes they do not.

Individual

In order for therapy to work, it requires vulnerability and emotional closeness between the child and their therapist. This can be inherently threatening to the parent. Why would they want to pay someone to have a close relationship with their child? In practice, therapists very rarely become closer to the child than his or her parents.

The most effective form of psychotherapy, as outlined previously, is relationship-based. But relationships have the power to both hurt and heal. When seeking a therapist for your child, inquire about the therapist's training in healing relationships. A windfall to engaging in relationship-based therapy is that it provides the child with an experience of a healthy relationship which can assist them as they mature and begin to make their own relationship choices.

Finally, sometimes individual therapy is insufficient; there are cases in which a child requires hospitalization or a residential placement. The typical progression is individual weekly psychotherapy, increasing its frequency, followed by considering a day psychiatric program, and lastly, a residential facility. Residential treatment can transform children's lives, but pose many ill side-effects. Of course, sometimes child behaviors can be so dangerous that they warrant immediate hospitalization. Nevertheless, if a child demonstrates this level of suffering, an individual therapist can assist families in navigating the appropriate level of care. Simply put, families need to maintain their authority, but sometimes the child's behavior demands an outside perspective.

Hybrid Family and Individual Therapy

Child-centered therapy is a hybrid form of relationship-based therapy. In this approach, the clinician meets with the child for the primary purpose of understanding his or her emotional worlds in an effort to assist his or her parents in better understanding their child's world (Ornstein, 1981). The assumption is that the child is having difficulties because his or her parents haven't been able to empathize with their child. There is a road block preventing empathy and the therapist can help the parents better empathize with their child, thus changing the emotional environment in the home and subsequently help bring everyone together. A potential pitfall to this approach is that it requires the parental investment and the therapist may inadvertently break the child's trust when speaking to the parents.

Although families naturally provide children with the ingredients required to develop and maintain their self-esteem, sometimes this process doesn't unfold naturally. When parenting a challenging child, professional consultation can be worth considering. Parents can increase a child's healthy idealization by setting firm limits, but this task can be counterintuitive for many adults. Secondly, empathy, arguably the opposite of limit setting, cannot be perfectly maintained, and children actually benefit from imperfect parenting. Additionally, belonging is important and your family's culture, traditions, and involvement in your community can play an integral part in the development of self-esteem. Finally, sometimes professional help is needed, but parenting is as human an activity as eating, drinking, and breathing. No one parents perfectly, and that's ok.

Healing the Self in the Home Case Study: Walter's Win

Walter was a friendly, thoughtful, and popular teenager. He dressed well and was a good-looking varsity athlete. Walter played soccer, basketball, and baseball. He didn't smoke cigarettes or use drugs, and only rarely snuck a Heineken from his family's refrigerator. He actively dated and periodically became consumed with intense romantic relationships. His family was successful, dedicated, kind, and loved him dearly. He had two older brothers and a younger sister who he respected and who also loved him. Despite this, Walter wanted to die.

On the surface, Walter had everything, so why did suicidal ideation haunt him? When his parents set reasonable limits, such as not allowing him to text his sweetheart or watch YouTube all night long, Walter flew into a rage. He screamed profanity and insults, punched walls, shattered windows, and threatened self-harm. Walter's family needed help.

The family looked for a therapist. They wanted someone who was smart— only the best for Walter. Initially, they found a young, newly graduated therapist, Ryan. Ryan was sincere and thoughtful, but brash and awkward. His borrowed office was simple and adorned with discount, warehouse furniture. The threadbare couch was lumpy and his desk was made of inexpensive pressboard. Unlike Walter's parents, Ryan didn't attend an elite college. Initially, Walter tried for a period with Ryan, but Ryan failed to impress Walter's parents. Quickly after beginning treatment, Walter's parents sought a more trained, better-experienced therapist.

Months later, Walter's parents called Ryan. Walter seemed to feel awful about himself, and his behavior had worsened. His parents wanted a consult with Ryan because Walter had mentioned he liked him; they thought it was worth a shot before admitting Walter to a treatment center. His parents said they couldn't stand to see him this upset; it broke their hearts. Walter's previous therapist had advised dropping him off at the well-known hospital and telling Walter that he wasn't welcome home until he straightened up.

Ryan, thought he may be able to help. Ryan met Walter's parents together. They were angry. Walter had been terrorizing them, and they desperately needed a break. "Walter needs to go; we can't take it anymore," they said.

Ryan breathed deeply as he listened to their frustrations. Walter was behaving badly. He snuck out of the house, smashed things, swore, was unruly, and was now physically aggressive toward his father. Ryan developed a plan. If Walter was willing, he would meet him, and periodically check-in with his parents. If he refused, he agreed to work solely with the parents.

Walter needed help quickly. But first, if his mom and dad truly believed that Walter was going to die, he had to be admitted to a hospital. Ryan explained that all therapeutic interventions had side effects. Even successful psychotherapy can communicate that the child is inherently flawed, broken, or possesses some defect that he or she has to work on forever. The potential benefits and side-effects of residential treatment are even greater. Going to a residential treatment center is like getting the word "shame" tattooed on your neck, except that only the child and his parents can read it. He further explained that he worked in residential treatment centers and believed in them, but warned about them. If they ended up taking Walter to a treatment center, he advised conveying the narrative that Walter forced his parents' hand, not that they abandoned him.

"If you skip this step," said Ryan, "think of every Thanksgiving dinner you will ever have again with your family. Imagine Walter looking across the table from you and knowing that you sent him away when he needed someone the most. Even if it works, it will change your family forever."

The family and Ryan developed a contract and discussed limit setting. There was going to be a single non-negotiable, absolute limit that violence wasn't tolerated. If Walter became physically aggressive, he would be admitted. Also, if, in the parents' judgment, or Ryan's, their son was actually going to kill himself, he would have to be hospitalized. In the meantime, mom and dad would strive to ignore the cursing, door slamming, and late-night texting, and they would give individual therapy with Ryan another try. Ryan attempted to have as little contact with the parents as possible and focused on building trust with Walter. If Walter didn't trust Ryan, little would change. If he thought Ryan was a spy, he wouldn't tell him much. If he did trust him, and began struggling with suicide, the trusting relationship would provide a measure of insurance.

Ryan and Walter met. Walter sat silently for the first few minutes. Ryan sat across from him, wondering if he was going to require hospitalization or residential treatment. Sitting in silence, a country music song came to Ryan's mind:

> "I hear the train a coming
> It's rolling round the bend
> And I ain't seen the sunshine since I don't know when
> I'm stuck in Folsom Prison and time keeps dragging on
> But the train keeps a rolling on to San Antonio"
> (Cash, 2010)

Ryan broke the uncomfortable silence. Ryan: "Walter, does this feel like prison?"

Walter: Yeah, man!
Ryan: That stinks. . . . What's on your mind?
Walter: Ok. . . .

Ryan and Walter were off. Ryan did his best to understand Walter, to listen and provide him a place to feel his complex, troubling feelings. Walter's job was to honestly say whatever came to mind, no matter how weird. Walter liked Ryan and the two began meeting weekly. Over time, Walter's misbehavior waned, he settled down, and he began to wrestle with typical difficulties that define adolescence.

Ryan, with Walter's permission, checked in with Walter's parents. Ryan explained to the parents that perhaps Walter was texting his girlfriend all throughout the night, not just to disobey his parents, but as an attempt to meet his need for closeness. Perhaps Walter "needed" to stay in close contact with her to reassure himself that she still cared about him. He suggested that Walter couldn't yet hold her in his mind. In this way, Ryan attempted to help Walter's parents understand Walter's perspective.

But Ryan struggled with the initial treatment question: Why did Walter want to kill himself? His parents were smart, empathic, loving, in-tune, and provided him a comfortable lifestyle. Walter was handsome and well-liked by his classmates. Why had he been so angry and suicidal?

Walter's parents called Ryan, stating that they were happy with Walter's progress, but were becoming increasingly concerned about next year's high school graduation. Walter's grades were lackluster and his SAT scores were moderate at best. That's when it occurred to Ryan—Walter's parents were brilliant. His father had an advanced graduate degree from a top university, won awards for his innovation, and had been a champion athlete at the highest level. His mother was articulate, poised, and had also graduated from an elite university. Walter clearly admired his parents, who were very empathic. Perhaps Walter felt he didn't belong. Arguably, Walter's immediate family was comprised of superstars and maybe Walter just felt average.

In the next session, Walter confessed that he felt that he could never gain acceptance to the type of schools where his family studied, and that he was never going to be as good an athlete as his father. Walter didn't feel that he measured up, so why bother?

Weeks later, his parents wanted to check-in with Ryan. After gaining Walter's permission, Ryan met with his parents and disclosed his hypothesis. Maybe Walter felt average. At the same time, his parents had wanted Ryan to review some testing that Walter had completed. Walter's testing indicated that his cognitive ability was average. In other words, Walter *felt* average and, if the testing was accurate, his academic potential was similar.

Perhaps Walter was typical, but his parents were atypical. Ryan explained the hypothesis using the statistical principle of regression to the mean. This is the mathematic principle that unusually high or low scores, when measured again, are likely to be closer to the mean or average. This is partly due to chance. His parents instantly understood. Maybe his parents were the outliers, but Walter didn't have a strong enough sense of belonging within his own family.

Walter's parents assured Ryan that they didn't knowingly pressure Walter into applying to an elite college. They just wanted him to be happy, contribute to society, and be a functioning adult. Any pressure that Walter experienced was of his own making. Walter's sense of otherness was deep, and perhaps he was using his selection of colleges to show his family how different he felt.

Walter kept working with Ryan, but it became clear that Walter felt less pressured and better understood by his family. Although Walter continued to require professional support, he felt much more like his family and much less like an outsider. Walter was neither a gifted student nor a national champion, but he utilized his talents the best way he could and easily won a place at the family table.

Discussion

Walter needed to belong. In his case, he found belonging with Ryan, and his family was able to recognize that he wasn't, in some ways, like them. His parents and siblings unknowingly expected Walter to have the same outstanding natural abilities. Initially, Ryan wasn't a "good enough" therapist; Walter's parents wanted someone better. When Walter's parents agreed to work with Ryan, it required them to stretch themselves to accommodate their son's preferences. In this way, the parents accepting Ryan predicted their capacity to accept their son.

Interestingly, Ryan's personal story was similar to Walter's. Ryan had grown up in an educated and demanding home. Ryan had often experienced not fitting in to his own family, who had discouraged his profession. Ryan never mentioned this similarity to Walter or his family, but the lived experiences of the therapist as well as the therapist's implicit qualities influence the treatment (Perlitz, 2019).

Walter needed to belong and when he stretched himself, his mother and father stretched themselves, too. They all found a place to meet, and Walter matured, to his parent's relief.

Ryan attempted to take an empathic stance with Walter. When he daydreamed of Johnny Cash it provided him a form of "data." Not that this data directly pertained to Walter, but for some reason, Ryan thought of a song about prison. Ryan didn't disclose to Walter what he was thinking, but rather wondered if he could form his own daydreams into an empathic hypothesis that Walter could confirm or deny. When Ryan asked Walter if he felt like the session was a prison, he was trying to demonstrate to Walter how he wished to encourage him to guide his own therapy. Ryan wanted to convey to Walter that he could tell him anything, even that his hypothesis was wrong. Maybe Ryan's guess was right and Walter really did feel incarcerated. Maybe Walter stretched himself and his acceptance of Ryan's empathic interpretation communicated that Walter was willing to accommodate Ryan. Either way, Walter agreed to meet with Ryan and avoided going to residential treatment.

Learning Activities

What values as a parent do you want for your children? What is important to you as you teach, guide, and assist your child into maturing as a functional adult? Write one or two paragraphs regarding your values and share them with your spouse or parenting partner. Does he or she share the same values?

Application Activities

Think about your childhood. What traits of your parents did you admire? Can you recall an instance where they were empathic towards your needs? Did it assist in helping you feel valued and cherished by them? If you are a parent now, think of how you could set and hold limits. Are there aspects of yourself that you believe your children idealize? Take a moment to write a paragraph or two characterizing your own parenting style. As you write, think of ways you do or would want to incorporate aspects of Healing the Self into your parenting.

References

Cash, J. (2010). *Johnny Cash sings Folsom Prison Blues*. Memphis, TN: Sun Records.

Deutsch, H. (1942). Some forms of emotional disturbance and their relationship to Schizophrenia. *The Psychoanalytic Quarterly*, *11*(3), 301–321. doi: https://doi.org/10.1080/21674086.1942.11925501

Doctors, S. (2017). Brandchaft's pathological accommodation—What it is and what it isn't, *psychoanalysis. Self and Context*, *12*(1), 45–59. doi:10.1080/15551024.2017.1251184

Elison, M. (1987). *The Kohut seminars: On self psychology with adolescents and young adults*. New York, NY: W.W. Norton and Company.

Kohut, H. (1968). The psychoanalytic treatment of narcissistic personality disorders. In *The Search for the Self* (Vol. I, pp. 477–509). New York, NY: International University Press.

Kohut, H. (1971). *The analysis of the self: A systematic approach to the psychoanalytic treatment of narcissistic personality disorders*. Madison, WI: International University Press.

Miller, A. (2008). *The drama of the gifted child: The search for the true self*. New York, NY: Basic Books.

Ornstein, A. (1981). Self-pathology in childhood. *Psychoanalytic Study of the Child*, *8*, 111–126.

Ornstein, A. (1981). Self-pathology in childhood: Developmental and clinical considerations. *Psychiatric Clinics of North America*, *4*(3), 435–453.

Perlitz, D. (2019). The implicit analyst: Qualities of Salience, Psychoanalysis, Self and Context. Advance online publication. doi: 10.1080/24720038.2019.1596272

Sherwood, V., & Cohen, C. (1994). *Psychotherapy of the quiet borderline patient. The as-if personality revisited*. New York, NY: Jason Aronson, Inc.

Winnicott, D. (1953). Transitional objects and transitional phenomena: A study of the first not-me possession. *International Journal of Psychoanalysis*, *34*(2), 89–97.

Winnicott, D. W. (1965). *The maturational processes and the facilitating environment: Studies in the theory of emotional development*. Oxford, England: International Universities Press.

aining Examples—Healing
: Self in Psychotherapy

This chapter includes case studies of the Healing the Self model used in therapy settings. The psychotherapy examples include Sam, a teenager struggling with low self-esteem; Johnny, an angry high schooler; and Mario, a student suffering from suicidal ideation. Each case highlights the Healing the Self relational ingredients of idealization, empathy, and belonging. Although each example attempts to dissect the three relational components, in practice these interventions are interwoven. That is, empathy and admiration generally foster closeness.

In the Healing the Self model, change occurs through closeness with another. This closeness lends itself to aspects of the therapist and the therapy becoming an important part of a child's development. That is, the sole therapeutic task is to become emotionally closer. In all treatment cases we will explore in this chapter, the therapist never directly addressed any thoughts, behaviors, or symptoms. Rather, in each of the cases, the therapist allowed the child to lead the way while putting faith in the relational model itself to facilitate lasting change.

These three therapy cases are included only to demonstrate how Healing the Self can be used by a trained therapist in a highly structured way. They are not intended to imply that adults in other roles, such as in classrooms, can or should attempt to use the model in the ways outlined in these case stories, but only that this is a possible application of the Healing the Self model. As training examples, these cases are subdivided into idealization, empathy, and belonging to demonstrate each concept as they are used in the therapy session. The stories use original language and Johnny's case has strong violent themes. All names have been changed to protect privacy.

Sam the Artist, Not the Athlete

Sam was a fifteen-year-old high school student who came to the school's counseling center seeking emotional support and saying that he needed someone to talk to about issues he couldn't tell his mother. He began meeting with Mr. M, a therapist trained in the Healing the Self model.

Sam told Mr. M that he had felt stressed and worried for quite a while. He said his father, George, expected more academically and athletically from him than Sam felt he could deliver. Linda, his mother, concurred, stating that Sam's father placed exceptionally high standards on Sam, but that they were both concerned about his poor academic performance. She further disclosed that Sam had previously been in counseling with a psychologist but that Sam said the psychologist "didn't understand."

Sam had a slight build and seemed smaller than average for a high school sophomore. He was a mediocre student, struggling to remain in the college track at his high school. Neither of Sam's parents attended a traditional university themselves so they very much wanted Sam to do so. In an attempt to feel more powerful and deal with his low self-esteem, Sam played football on his school's team as a defensive lineman. His small frame ensured that Sam got knocked around and beat up a lot during games, but he gave football his all.

Sam was the oldest of three children. He had a younger sister, Mindy, age 13, and a brother, Chris, age 11. Sam was very close to his siblings, especially Chris, who suffered from Autism Spectrum Disorder. The children's parents had divorced when Sam was six and now equally shared custody, rearing, and parental responsibilities. Linda explained that she and Sam's father had a good relationship, though George suffered from untreated depression. Sam's paternal grandfather died by suicide before Sam was born. Linda had remarried, and two years before, divorced. She was currently taking classes at the local community college and dating. Sam shared that he and his mother's ex-husband "didn't see eye-to-eye."

During one of the initial counseling sessions, Sam asked Mr. M a specific question about football—he wondered if Mr. M liked Tom Brady. The therapist decided to avoid answering the question as part of his initial therapeutic approach to Sam. Mr. M then wondered if Sam saw through his attempt to hide his nearly complete ignorance of professional sports. Mr. M immediately sensed a divide between them. Sam again pushed the sports line of questioning by asking Mr. M if he had a favorite basketball player. Mr. M initially responded by asking Sam if he was wondering if he could trust Mr. M, or if he was a good enough therapist to help him. Sam shook his head, and the divide widened.

To help narrow the gap that had developed between them, Mr. M told Sam that he was once close friends with someone who played in the NBA. Sam smiled and said excitedly, "It's cool that you have a friend who used to play in the NBA!" Sam then asked Mr. M if he played any sports. Mr. M told him that he did not, but that he used to run road races. Sam then looked around the office and noticed a running photograph and said, "Cool." Mr. M asked Sam if this was what he wanted to talk about. He smiled and instead began talking about his frustrations with his brother Chris.

In a following session, Sam told Mr. M he was excited about his grades and anticipated that he might make the honor roll. Grades had always been an issue for him and he was very pleased that the honor roll seemed to finally be within reach. During the session, however, Sam also admitted that he had done poorly on a math exam, which worried him. Once home, he confessed this to his mother and told her he feared he might no longer be in the running to make the honor roll. By Sam's account, his mother had little faith that this academic year would be any different from previous ones and seemed to doubt his ability to make improvement. Sam's sister, Mindy, then entered the room and began gloating over her certainty of making the honor roll. Sam said that he became enraged and ran from the room as he fantasized about punching Mindy in the face.

Later, when Sam told Mr. M about this encounter at home, Sam looked angry. His body tensed, his brow furrowed, and the inflection in his voice changed. Sam was enraged. "Mom doesn't know how important getting on the honor roll is to you," Mr. M ventured. Immediately Sam relaxed. Mr. M said, "She doesn't know how hard you have been working." Quickly thereafter, Sam admitted that he did not really want to hit his sister and that she wouldn't have teased him if she had known the extent of his effort. He appeared calmer, his anger gone. Mr. M hypothesized that most of Sam's frustration came about because he didn't feel he had enough worth in the eyes of his parents. A lack of self-esteem had Sam worried and anxious and expending tons of energy on sports and athletics in a misguided attempt to feel like he belonged.

At the next session with Mr. M, Sam disclosed his feelings for a girl he fancied, and talked about his school schedule, and how he got into several of the classes that he wanted. In an effort to help Sam feel understood, Mr. M smiled warmly and said, "That's awesome!" Sam smiled back and then reported that for the first time his father had taken him out driving. As Sam spoke, his demeanor began to lighten. Eventually, Sam laughed and shared that he was so nervous to be behind the wheel that he had not driven faster than 20 miles per hour. He then smiled and said driving was awesome. He elaborated that on the road, by happenstance, he saw the girl he liked from school, who was also learning to drive. He said that at one point they were both on the same road and that she was coming toward him from the opposite direction. He grinned, explaining that they were both so nervous that they passed each other moving like turtles, hugging the right-side shoulder. As Sam spoke, Mr. M leaned forward and matched Sam's toothy grin, and after Sam had finished telling his story, they both laughed. Sam relaxed in his chair and grinned contently.

Mr. M continued to work with Sam to build his self-esteem by taking an empathic approach to Sam's relationship problems with his parents and by mostly listening to Sam as he poured out his feelings. As his sessions with Mr. M progressed, Sam began to exhibit more confidence. He made new friends and his grades improved. He no longer needed his anger and anxiety to deal with his feelings of inadequacy. He admitted to Mr. M that he had been thinking about participating in activities other than football, and was contemplating taking some art classes. Mr. M was encouraging as he talked with Sam about these new pursuits and pleased to hear that Sam seemed to be gaining a better sense of self—a sense that was giving him the courage to find out more about who he really was.

In one of their final sessions, Sam talked about a mythology class he was taking and how he asked his teacher if the class could watch *A Hitch-hikers Guide to the Galaxy* for an in-class project on modern folklore. Sam explained that in the film, the greatest of all computers answers the question of the meaning of life. However, the computer takes seven and half million years to compute and respond, and by the time it reveals the long-sought answer everyone has forgotten the question! Sam explained to Mr. M that the answer the computer gives to the question about the meaning of life is "42," which makes no sense. Then Sam spoke about his mother's boyfriend, and how he enjoyed talking to him about philosophy and the meaning of life. In the last few moments of the session, Sam disclosed that in therapy he had been able to figure out the questions in his life then asked if Mr. M knew the answers to Sam's questions. Mr. M smiled at Sam warmly but didn't answer. Then Sam laughed and told him that he knew what Mr. M was thinking . . . he was thinking of the number 42. Mr. M chuckled and told Sam that he was pretty clever. What is noteworthy about this incident is not that Sam correctly assumed what Mr. M was thinking, but that Sam may have experienced a psychic merging with Mr. M. That is, he experienced connectedness, which was something Sam desperately needed in order to build his self-esteem.

The close relationship between Sam and Mr. M was healing for Sam. It gave him the courage to let go of his anger and insecurities. As his anger waned, he was able to access his more vulnerable, artistic side and to hunker down academically. He decided to quit playing football his junior year and focus instead on his artistic talents, which he realized were his true gift. Sam's grades improved so much that by the time he graduated he was college bound. Through connections at his school, his considerable artistic talent began to be recognized and promoted. Within a year of graduation Sam was touring internationally and showcasing his artwork in prestigious exhibits throughout Europe.

Discussion

One of the goals Mr. M had in working with Sam was to provide him a place where he could deeply connect with another person. Mr. M did this by continuously trying to understand Sam's world and, by doing so, helped Sam co-create new meanings. Meaning is important because it defines emotional pain.

The experience of "clicking" with someone is created not just through language but through the countless interactions between therapist and patient (Wolf, 1988). In the simplest terms, therapy helps someone feel human in a human world. When seen through this lens, Sam's feelings of anger and anxiety could be compounded by problems of not feeling like he fit with his family. That is, perhaps his feelings of worry were because he didn't feel he belonged. Ironically, independence and fully developed self-esteem both require a sense of belonging. Given that human infants must feel known in a human environment in order to develop as a person, it was Mr. M's goal to become emotionally close to Sam so that he could hold him in his mind (Kohut, 1984). Sam appeared to be settled and grounded by the experience of feeling recognized and accepted by someone emotionally close to him. Sam's increased openness and comfort in therapy indicated emotional growth and a greater sense of self. As a result, Sam seemed to worry less, be more flexible with others, and was better able to use his considerable energy for learning.

Idealization

There are many forms of therapy in which the therapist refrains from answering questions. This is because feelings are based on both reality and the imagination. When a therapist answers questions, it can remove the imagination, but increase the closeness. But Mr. M felt a huge divide between himself and Sam when he failed to answer Sam's question regarding football. However, by honestly answering his question about basketball and sharing his involvement in running, Mr. M was able to bring the two of them closer and it was easier for Sam to look up to him. This idealization is important because without it, Mr. M's attempts at validating Sam's developmental milestones would be of limited value. Sam needed someone he perceived could help him. In order for the therapy to make a difference for Sam, Mr. M had to be someone Sam could admire. By asking Mr. M to share his perspective on a topic that was important to him, Sam was in a sense fishing for an opportunity to admire his therapist. Once Mr. M was able to begin meeting this need, Sam could start the process of sharing his experience with some hope of feeling appreciably validated.

Empathy

Aggression is an attempt to heal self-esteem, which becomes threatened when children feel misunderstood. Rather than discussing Sam's aggressive feelings toward his sister when he thought about punching her, Mr. M took an empathic stance when he stated that Sam's mom didn't understand how important his grades were to him. This was an attempt to use empathy to help Sam feel understood, thereby reducing his wish to hit his sister. Specifically, verbal validation helped Sam feel whole and thus he didn't need to become angry. Following Mr. M's empathy, Sam smiled in what felt like a comfortable silence for several minutes.

Validating developmental milestones is a hallmark of empathy and imperative for strengthening a sense of self. Arguably, learning to drive a car could be understood as an important developmental task for an adolescent. Therefore, it was important for Mr. M to validate Sam's attempts at learning this developmental skill, which he did by mirroring Sam's body language, leaning into him, and matching his smile.

Through the use of empathy and mirroring, Mr. M attempted to carefully enter Sam's subjective world in an effort to help him feel understood. That is, he tried to feel what it would be like to register for high school classes, drive a car for the first time, and begin to form a crush. This required that Mr. M lower his own emotional boundaries and try to see and explore the world as Sam did. By validating Sam's affect, specifically his excitement about getting the classes he wanted, the approach may have encouraged him to share about his driving lesson, thereby further establishing a sense of trust and being known.

Belonging

Sam and Mr. M became a team. Mr. M strove to understand and connect with Sam, and Sam did the hard work of allowing himself to be known. When both knew that the other was thinking of 42, it was a sign that Sam and Mr. M were in tune. In a sense, Sam felt like he belonged to Mr. M. In therapy, Sam allowed himself to be truly vulnerable with his therapist and did the hard work of honestly speaking his mind and sharing his shortcomings. This vulnerability permitted him to develop a sense of belonging with Mr. M.

Johnny's Rifle

Important Note: This is a multi-year intensive psychotherapy treatment case with an experienced doctoral-level clinical psychologist. This student was treated in highly structured psychotherapy with multiple supports for the student, therapist, and the school community. If a student threatens any violence, please follow your district's policies and immediately contact your supervisor. This case study has strong violent themes. It is included in the book only to demonstrate an extreme application of the Healing the Self model. In no way can a teacher be expected or asked to provide this level of psychotherapy. Please read it only in an effort to better understand the importance of healthy idealization, empathy, and belonging and nothing more.

Karin was a licensed, highly experienced therapist with additional training in Healing the Self. She was contacted to assess a new student, Johnny, and assist in designing an individual educational plan that best met his needs. Karin met with Johnny's new teachers and the special education director to discuss these needs. Johnny was a fifteen-year-old who wrote at between a third and fourth grade level. Despite being bright, he suffered from dyslexia. Tall and very thin, he walked on his toes. He seemed angry and depressed. Johnny was told by his mother that he was going on vacation, when in fact he was being moved to live with a distant family member who could supposedly straighten him out. Johnny had come from a large, metropolitan area to a small, rural community and a tiny high school. His new town had a country store, post office, and not much else. He moved away from his mother and a close, but not necessarily positive, neighborhood peer group. His new school for seventh to twelfth graders, though small, prided itself on its ability to help struggling students catch up.

At an initial meeting, which Karin attended to presumably review additional reading supports, Johnny moped his way up to the meeting table. He carried a "just beat it attitude" with him. His head down, a Chevy baseball cap and a black hooded sweatshirt partially concealed his face. Johnny coldly stared through his teachers and special education support people. One of the special education teachers commented that the hair stood up on the back of his neck when he worked with Johnny. It immediately became clear that this student required more than reading support. Johnny's cold stare frightened his classmates.

Johnny loved guns. He studied them and was outwardly obsessed with them. He carried *Guns and Ammo* and different para-military type magazines with him. In a misguided effort to impress his classmates, he talked at length about how many guns he owned or had fired. He quickly alienated the liberal school culture and distanced himself from everyone. Although he never threatened staff, he'd say things like, "You know a nine-millimeter Luger round won't blow out the back of a human head, but will rip through a skull and bounce around a human brain."

Karin was asked to meet with Johnny one-on-one to perform a risk assessment to determine if he was going to open fire at the school. She was told he hated therapists. She sat in a windowless office waiting. A silver-haired, kind-hearted teacher brought Johnny to the door. "This is Johnny," he said. Johnny walked in and sat down gracefully, wearing all black and coolly staring into Karin's eyes. He sat directly across from her, their eyes level. It felt like a toe-to-toe boxing match. A cold, uncomfortable silence fell between them. Karin wondered if she was sitting across from a young man plotting to murder his classmates. Moments later, in an aggressive and demeaning tone, he said, "Let me ask you this, Doc. What am I thinking about right now? I'll give you a hint: it's a chair." Karin waited a moment then responded by saying, "It's the chair you're sitting in, which is just like mine." Johnny smiled and said, "You're right, Doc. How did you know?" Karin said, "Because it's just you and me. Reckon you could talk to someone like me?" Johnny said he thought maybe he could.

Karin believed that juvenile clients come to therapy in enough distress, so the therapist should always try to make things better for the child, and that there was no need to unlock deep material outside of the child's awareness. In fact, her stance was that the therapeutic task is to protect the child from too many strong, disorganizing feelings. These feelings are those that children need adults to understand and help them express. The job of therapy is to communicate that adults can protect children from emotions that are too powerful for them to handle alone. Moreover, kids will naturally become more vulnerable when they feel cared for and sense that someone has the capacity to deeply understand them. When someone feels understood, they let go a little bit (Stolorow, 2018). Karin thought of all this as she retreated into the safe library of her mind while sitting across from Johnny.

The rest of the session Johnny talked about guns—rifles, pistols, and machine guns. He showed Karin a tattered magazine that had an article demonstrating how to convert a briefcase to hide a submachine gun that allowed a secret agent to fire it unnoticed. He confided that he had read the article countless times. Karin didn't ask him what guns meant to him, but silently imagined. Karin told him they could talk about guns, but that they had to have an agreement that if he ever thought of hurting himself or others he had to call her, day or night. Karin told him if he called she would answer if she could and would immediately schedule a time to talk. The agreement felt weak and silly to her, but she felt the need to make it with him. Johnny and Karin then began meeting at the school once a week, which went on for three years.

Students, teachers, administrators, and his family were well aware of Johnny's outward anger and frustration, and his obsession with firearms. Subsequently, the school was quite happy that Karin and Johnny had begun working together. Teachers were scared that this strange, unknown kid could shoot someone. Although Johnny never made a direct threat, he was angry. His family was well aware of his gun talk and assured Karin that all firearms were secure and that Johnny had no access to any guns. But the school district's experienced special educator confided, "I'm terrified that he's going to snap."

Johnny wasn't a talker. In their first months working together, Johnny drew Karin maps of where he used to live and where he hid knives, swords, and weapons in his house in case he was attacked by a stranger. Karin asked Johnny if telling her this meant that a part of him strived to be a grown-up, responsible for his own life. He didn't respond. He showed Karin pictures of himself target shooting with high-power, military-type weapons with an adult. He made hints of having access to an armory of high-tech weaponry, but then always told her he was kidding. Karin recalled the old country saying, "Nothing is more serious than a joke about sex or violence." He asked Karin if she was going to "rat him out."

Karin left sessions terrified. Was Johnny testing her or did he really have a Glock automatic pistol and an AK-47? Karin sought and paid for weekly consultation from a highly experienced psychiatrist who had additional training in talk therapy. He was trained by a British therapist with a literature background. This psychiatrist taught Karin to listen for themes in what patients told her. Karin felt emotionally held by this psychiatrist when attempting to understand Johnny. In this way, she had backup and was less alone.

Sessions with Johnny were about guns, guns, and guns. Much like exotic car posters that some teenagers hang on their bedroom walls, Johnny loved exotic, expensive, German-made guns—the Porsches of guns. Karin tried to imagine how these guns held Johnny together. Did he feel weak, slow, boring? Was his wish to feel powerful, fast, and interesting? Karin kept these thoughts to herself. Johnny asked her, "Have you ever shot a gun?" Karin told Johnny that she was an avid deer hunter and knew about rifles. Karin then disclosed that she learned about guns at the FBI Academy in Quantico, Virginia, in a very different phase of her life. Johnny appeared relieved by her confession. He yearned to be both understood by her and have a sameness with her. Johnny then said, "Learning about guns from the FBI is cool."

As their work progressed, Karin learned that Johnny and his relative enjoyed target practice together. A part of Karin cringed when Johnny showed her pictures on his phone of him shooting pistols and an AK-47, presumably with a responsible adult.

One day, as Johnny sat down for their session, he placed his large backpack between them. There was an odd bulge in it. Together they both stared at it, periodically glancing at each other in silence. Johnny finally asked, "What do you think is in my backpack?" He waited for Karin's response. "It's a nightstick," Johnny said. "Cops use them. What did you think it was? Think I brought my AK!?" Karin said, "I'm glad you didn't." Both of them laughed out loud. It turned out that Johnny had participated in career day and had brought the nightstick to school. The administration knew he had it, and after their session Johnny was planning on putting it back in his car.

The more Johnny talked with Karin about Fabrique Nationale, Heckler and Koch, Sig Saur and other expensive guns, the less he talked about them in class. Johnny slowly began earning the trust of his teachers, who no longer feared him. He started talking to peers and joined a sports team. He grew taller, his chest filled out, and he walked down the hall with his head held high. He lost his sweatshirt and began wearing well-fitting, trendy clothes.

Karin and Johnny's work together continued over the next year and Karin continued to attempt to understand why Johnny needed the guns. Their sessions often had long periods of silence. Karin asked if the quiet drove him crazy, and he assured her that it did not. They spent many minutes happily sitting across from each other in silence, occasionally grinning. Johnny began smiling in class. Faculty no longer caught Karin in the hall to tell her some outlandish thing Johnny had said. He began sitting with other students in the cafeteria before school and during lunch. In session, he disclosed that he could be friends with "bongo-beating hippie liberals." Girls began to take an interest in him.

While things at school seemed to be getting better, Johnny's home life became increasingly difficult. His caregiver had multiple relationship complications. At one point, his caregiver promised Johnny a special hunting trip. He was excited and for weeks spoke at length about what to bring. Johnny wept when he learned that by "special trip" his caregiver meant drinking. The trip was a ruse for drinking beer with buddies. Johnny was so disappointed he didn't go. But through therapy with Karin, Johnny became increasingly real and vulnerable in sessions and talked less and less about guns. Instead, he began talking about his future and mustered the courage to explore some of the deep feelings of inadequacy that hold up identity formation.

Johnny turned eighteen and his interest in girls increased. He transformed from an awkward, self-conscious teenager to a handsome, strapping young man. Many girls became fond of him. But he wasn't interested in girls as objects; he was far more interested in developing real connections. He could talk about his feelings and would often, in session, explain how one girl wanted to go all the way with him, not to be closer but to hide her real self from him. Sex for many people, Johnny wondered, might be a way not to be known. It was a phony way of forcing someone into a routine that seemed real and close, but wasn't. Maybe sex could actually close doors to realness. Johnny talked openly about these topics with Karin. From their sessions it appeared that many classmates, both girls and boys, were eager to accept Johnny's advice on dating and life. Perhaps due to his work with Karin, Johnny could talk about how people hid themselves from others and being true to oneself took real courage.

Girls adored him. He had attended three proms in three different high schools and was careful to rent three different cummerbunds to match each of his dates' dresses. One of his dates was anti-gun, Johnny bashfully told Karin. He said there was a lot to not like about guns, and that it was "ok" that she had strong, differing opinions regarding firearms. Johnny cared deeply for others and wasn't afraid to show peers true concern.

Before what she thought was their last session together, Karin was driving in to her parking space at the school when she saw a fancy, souped-up sports car whip through the parking lot. Karin immediately pulled to the right to avoid the car and spilled steaming coffee all over her lap. Frustrated, she leapt from her car, angry and startled. The driver saw Karin, threw the car in reverse and recklessly drove up to her. It was Johnny. Karin said, "Johnny! Whose car is this!? Damn it, Johnny!" Johnny replied, "Doc. Relax. It's my new girlfriend's. She lent it to me. It's nice . . . check it out." Karin carefully opened the door and admired the leather interior with contrasting stitching. "Johnny, this is a nice car, man," she said. Johnny then asked, "Doc, I really need a Starbucks. Wanna go?" Karin said, "Thanks, but I'm wearing my coffee. I can't go with you. We still meeting?" Johnny replied, "Doubt it. I graduated and came by just to say bye."

In the parking lot, leaning on his borrowed rally car, Johnny and Karin laughed together as they said their goodbyes. Karin was proud of Johnny for graduating and told him that if things ever got hairy to give her a call. Johnny thanked her for listening and sped off recklessly.

Discussion

When Karin met Johnny, his self-esteem was rock bottom. He didn't feel connected, cared for, or worthy. Their work consisted of Karin attempting to deeply connect to him—thereby reducing his anger and violence potential—and the use of the three relational components needed to develop self-esteem: idealization, empathy, and belonging.

Johnny ultimately never hurt anyone. Although many of the signs were present, Karin believed that their work together enabled him to develop self-worth and possibly avoid a serious tragedy. Johnny's reading and writing improved. He graduated from high school after completing his final paper which explored a controversial public policy issue. As of this writing, he is seeking gainful employment in a needed trade. Johnny is happy, well-liked, and proud of himself. He has a vast social circle and reasonable expectations for himself and others.

Idealization

Johnny desperately needed an adult to look up to. He couldn't admire his mother, who sent him away, and for multiple reasons he couldn't admire the relative he was living with. His relative's "hunting trip" was a tremendous letdown. Johnny really wanted to go. Johnny couldn't easily admire his relative.

Johnny learned to admire Karin instead, a stable, caring adult who shared some of his interests and experiences. Johnny needed her to not be afraid of his threatening nature and love of guns. He needed her to be strong enough to care for him. Therapists and teachers often serve as the only stable, successful adult in students' lives. His relationships with Karin and several of his teachers showed Johnny that adults and adulthood could be different from what he had experienced up to that point.

Lacking adults to idealize (and keep him safe and secure from an early age), Johnny learned to idealize guns. Johnny didn't lust after a new deer hunting rifle, but high-tech complicated, military style guns. He wasn't satisfied with typical sporting arms; they had to be special because Johnny himself felt so lackluster. His idealization of guns reached to the level of obsession because a healthy idealization of a role model was missing in his life. He tried to elevate himself by associating himself with elite, special weaponry.

Empathy

Johnny needed Karin to understand him and feel with him, to imagine what it would be like to move to a new region of the country, be alone, and feel deeply misunderstood. Rather than seeing his target practice as bad, Karin attempted to take an empathic stance and understand it from Johnny's perspective. Although frightening to Karin, for Johnny shooting meant that he was a powerful man, a grown-up—target practice gave him a way to strive for maturity. For Johnny, target practice meant that he wanted to control his own life and become a responsible adult. When Karin validated his experience and feelings, directly and indirectly, Johnny felt understood and cared for, something desperately lacking in his life. Their empathic connection was new information for Johnny: he learned that his thoughts and feelings mattered . . . that he mattered. Over time he was able to internalize this and develop into a confident, stable young man.

Belonging

When Johnny asked Karin in their first session if she knew what he was thinking and provided her a hint about the chair, Karin believed that he was seeking emotional closeness with her and a sense of belonging. He wanted her to "read his mind" and know him with the closeness that infants have with their parents—a oneness with another human that is so important, but primitive, that language can't capture it. Johnny drew pictures for Karin because he wanted her to see his house and his room as if she lived there, too. He longed for her to be so close that they shared the same mind.

It was vital that Johnny felt Karin wanted to be part of his life (the opposite of most of his adult relationships). By inviting him to call her anytime, Karin was teaching Johnny that he belonged. By showing up for their appointments and being interested in his interests, Karin made it possible for Johnny to let his protective guard down and to be able to relax enough to discover his true self. This closeness also helped Johnny feel that he felt he belonged, not just with Karin and their meetings, but in his new school, among his new peer group. He had to feel wanted and cared about before he could allow himself to tolerate the uncertainties of teenage socialization.

To summarize the training examples used thus far in the chapter, Sam was a teenager who needed more confidence and who struggled with modest issues of anger. Johnny's struggles terrified the school. Although at different places on the continuum of suffering, both teenagers benefited from the Healing the Self model. Sam found his true calling as an artist and got along better at home. Johnny never hurt anyone and changed from an awkward, angry young man to one of the most popular students in the school.

Mario's Sessions

"We're really concerned. We don't know much about this kid, except that he just got out of the psychiatric hospital for suicidal ideation. He's anxious and can't be around other students. Moreover, there are medical needs and the sending hospital hasn't sent us much to work on. We need a game plan," the school's special services director told Peter.

The initial game plan was to use a private office and free up a talented educational support person, Donald, to tutor him for a shortened, three-hour school a day. The two would get to know each other, and once Mario felt more comfortable at school, the school would carefully increase his exposure. In the meantime, the school provided a comprehensive psychological evaluation to better understand his cognitive strengths, achievement levels, and social/emotional functioning.

In a pale blue, windowless office, Donald and Mario sat together. Mario was quiet. Donald outlined the day's studies. A page from an old academic achievement test that pictured the iconic pre-9/11 Twin Towers hung on the wall. Donald had the door open in case there was a problem. Mario quietly listened as Donald gave the reading assignment. In the coming weeks, a psychologist completed a psychological assessment.

Mario's assessment indicated that many of his academic skills were actually superior to his cognitive abilities. In other words, Mario gave his academics his all. His cognitive scores were scattered. On some tasks, his performance was average, on others very low. His visual spatial skills and working memory were strong, whereas his ability to solve nonverbal problems was low, along with his verbal skills. Mario didn't think in words. He thought with his hands and eyes. During the assessment, the psychologist noted that Mario appeared very anxious and obsessive. He arranged the testing materials perfectly before starting the assessment and demanded that the evaluator neatly line-up the pencils that the pair used. Everything had to be perfect.

At about the same time, Mario met his therapist, Peter. Peter was a school therapist assigned to Mario though his Individual Education Plan (IEP). Peter met Mario in a small office next to the study hall. Peter instantly liked Mario. For therapy to be useful, it's best if the couple authentically likes one another. If the therapist consistently tries to fake his or her interest in the patient, growth rarely occur (McWilliams, 2004). Interestingly, the brain scientist Mark Solms believes that as we discover more and more sophisticated tools for exploring the human brain, we may better understand the neurological underpinnings for what enables people to click with one another (Solms, 2015). Most importantly, Mario seemed to like Peter, too.

Peter had been introduced to the Healing the Self model and decided to play with its ideals. At the start of the first session, Peter asked Mario if he had been to therapy before. Mario answered he had. Peter then explained the limits of confidentially. "Unless it hurts you, another kid, or an old person, I'll never rat you out. Never!" Peter explained. Mario nodded and said, "Yeah. Hey, can we play cards?"

"Sure." Peter shuffled the red poker cards seven times to ensure randomness. Mario then taught Peter how to play Gin Rummy. Mario stacked his completed card sets ("books") perfectly straight. Then he asked Peter about his weekend, which Peter answered was, "Ok, typical, some reading and writing." The remainder of the hour was spent quietly playing cards. The therapy hour ended and Mario agreed to meet the following week.

The next week, Mario came five minutes early. Mario began the session by asking about Peter's weekend and if they could play cards. Peter answered about his weekend and shuffled the cards exactly seven times. The two played cards quietly. Halfway through the session, Peter broke the silence. "You know Mario, I will never rat you out." "Yeah. I know," Mario said. Peter asked nothing of Mario. Mario said little.

The following sessions were very much the same. Mario asked Peter about his weekend, Peter answered. Mario asked to play cards. Peter shuffled seven time, they played cards, and Peter reminded Mario, "I will never rat you out." Mario responded, "Yeah."

At the same time, Mario's teachers reported that Mario seemed far less anxious at school. His school day was lengthened. He began taking a vocational class with other students, which went well. Within weeks, Mario transitioned to a typical school day.

Mario remained in therapy with Peter. The sessions were now nearly identical:

1. Mario arrived five minutes early.
2. Mario asked Peter about his weekend and asked to play cards.
3. Peter shuffled the deck seven times.
4. The two played Gin Rummy.
5. Peter reminded Mario he would, "Never rat him out."
6. Mario answered, "Yeah."

It is important to note that Peter asked Mario no direct questions. He refrained from asking him about suicidal ideation, his family dynamics, his mood, his physical health, friends, or even his academics. Rather, Peter trusted that Mario knew what Mario needed. Peter believed that he didn't have a God's-eye view of the therapy or even that he somehow knew what Mario needed better than Mario did. By trusting Mario, Peter hoped to demonstrate that Mario was worthy of trust.

Mario asked Peter to meet over the summer. Again, the sessions were essentially identical. The school year began and again they met. Each session was exactly the same.

Then entered AC/DC.

Mario asked Peter if they could listen to rock-n-roll. Peter agreed, and the sessions then included loud AC/DC music. Although Mario seemed to greatly enjoy listening to rock, it is important to note that the teachers in the neighboring study hall did not share Mario's newfound enthusiasm for AC/DC. Sessions then followed a new sequence:

1. Mario arrived early.
2. Mario asked Peter about his weekend and asked to play cards.
3. Peter shuffled the deck seven times.
4. The two played Gin Rummy.
5. They listened to AC/DC.

    a. "Highway to Hell"
    b. "Back in Black"
    c. "Shoot to Thrill"
    d. "Hells Bells"
    e. Etc.

6. Peter reminded Mario he would "never rat him out."
7. Mario answered, "Yeah."

While listening to AC/DC, Mario asked if Peter had to shuffle the cards seven times. "Of course, it's the only way to ensure they are perfectly random." Was Mario, in his way, asking Peter to change? Was this a critique of Peter's perfectionism? Was Peter mirroring Mario's obsessive tendencies? Peter laid the cards on the table and scooped them up rather than shuffling them.

The next session was different. This time, Mario asked to play Monopoly. The two played the game together, and while putting the game back in the box, again Peter reminded Mario, "I will never rat you out."

At Mario's teachers' requests, and with Mario's consent, Peter met with Mario's educational team as part of the IEP process. Mario was well-liked, his grades were strong, and his teachers reported no concerns. In fact, Mario had become a leader among his peers, and other students admired him. He even started a popular after-school club. Moreover, Mario earned acceptance to a four-year college. By all accounts, Mario was doing well and the educational team suggested ending the therapy.

In the next session, Mario arrived early. The session began following the pattern, but this time, Peter contaminated the sequence. Peter asked if Mario ever thought about ending their work together. Mario snapped back, "I know we can talk about anything, but not that." During the session, Mario and Peter were eventually able to discuss termination. The two agreed to end their treatment following Mario's graduation. Again, Peter reminded Mario, "I will never rat you out."

In the following session, Mario wanted to return to cards. Peter shuffled the deck once, with Mario's completed books hastily jumbled on the table. Then Mario brought out the game that he wanted to play with Peter. In the new game, Mario was a master and thrashed Peter. Peter wasn't skilled at the game. Mario guided him and taught him how to play. At the sessions end, Peter again reminded Mario, "I will never rat you out." Mario responded, "You know, I believe you."

Discussion

This case is incomplete and carries multiple mysteries. Why didn't Mario talk? Was playing cards and other games a silent collusion that what Mario wanted to say was, in fact, too scary or shameful to say? Was nearly silent therapy useful, even ethical? How did Mario get better?

Relationships are the mechanism that enable a child to grow self-esteem. Self-esteem enables children to control feelings both pleasant and unpleasant. When the child is able to absorb the relationship into his or her mind, then the foundation is made for lasting self-esteem. One way to consider Peter's and Mario's therapy is that Peter attempted to become close to Mario at an intimate, preverbal level.

Idealization

By not asking Mario any questions about his experience, Peter was attempting to communicate that he wasn't scared of Mario. Peter wanted Mario to lead the way and felt confident that Mario authentically did know what was best. Who was Peter to prioritize his wish of what therapy could be? The old critique is that therapists force patents to have therapeutic experiences that match their own. Perhaps Mario admired Peter's restraint.

Empathy

There are different schools of thought regarding a therapist reading a patient's psychological evaluation. Some thinkers believe, of course, that the therapist should learn as much as they can about the patient. For example, the therapist might take a detailed personal history and contact the patient's physician. On the other hand, some believe that the therapist should meet and work with the patient without any information that the patient doesn't provide. This school believes that therapy must be symbolic, so the "facts" of the matter are only a distraction. By reading Mario's psychological evaluation, Peter placed himself in the first camp. He wondered if mainly using words, a primary tool of therapy, would distance himself from Mario (Wachtel, 2008). In a way, Peter attempted to engage Mario where he was. Mario didn't rely on words, so for the 50-minute session, neither did Peter. This was Peter's attempt at taking an empathic stance with Mario.

Belonging

"It is a joy to be hidden but a disaster not to be found" (Winnicott, 1965, p. 187). Mario needed someone who would follow his lead and look for him, rather than impose their vision of health upon him. Parents, teachers, and therapists know this concept well. Grown-ups working with children know that kids require empathic understanding while envisioning the child's potential. By listening to Mario and not "forcing" him to talk, Mario felt understood, and the foundation necessary for a sense of belonging was created. Peter, a talker by trade, had to develop a silent ritual that he and Mario could share.

Generally, therapists use the patient's disclosures to track if the therapy is helpful. In Mario's case, Peter couldn't have known if it was working, except that Mario's grades improved, teachers reported no problems, and there was no indication of suicidality. It would be difficult to claim, however, that the all of Mario's growth resulted from his sessions with Peter. We do know that they had a private language and after their time together, Mario was happy, loved life, and perhaps was found.

References

Kohut, H. (1984). The self-psychological approach to defense and resistance. In Goldberg (Ed.) *How does analysis cure?* (pp. 13–33). Chicago, IL: University of Chicago Press.

McWilliams, N. (2004). *Psychoanalytic psychotherapy: A practitioner's guide.* New York, NY: Guilford Press.

Solms, M. (2015). *The feeling brain: Selected papers on neuropsychoanalysis.* New York, NY: Routledge.

Stolorow, R. (2018). Emotional disturbance, trauma, and authenticity: A phenomenological-contextualist psychoanalytic perspective. In K. Aho, (Ed.), *Existential medicine: Essays on health and illness* (pp.12–25). London, England: Rowman and Littlefield International.

Wachtel, P. (2008). *Relational theory and the practice if psychotherapy.* New York, NY: Guilford Press.

Winnicott, W. (1965). *Playing and reality.* New York, NY: Routledge.

Wold, E. S. (1988). *Treating the self: Elements of clinical self psychology.* New York, NY: Guilford Press.

12 Vignettes and Learning Activities

This chapter provides brief case illustrations of how the Healing the Self model can be used in specific interventions targeted to meeting children's relational needs in an effort to nurture their sense of self. The examples range from educational to clinical settings. Following each vignette is a brief quiz regarding the specific intervention used to help the child grow or were important for understanding the child's challenges. Write your answers and learn how they compare to the Learning Discussion Points section.

1) Ninja Teacher: School Setting

Martin was a seventeen-year-old suffering from an emotional disturbance. He had a history of violent crime, incarceration, and gang affiliation. Martin was large for his age and had been expelled from high school for fist fighting and throwing chairs. He was significantly behind his grade level in reading. On the first day of school at a new alternative high school he had been enrolled in, Martin became very upset and screamed at his teacher. He was then asked to go to the time-out room to cool down. The time-out room was a large classroom with no wall décor and just a single chair. Martin happily walked himself to the room, swung open the door, and slammed it shut. In the room, Martin's disruptive behavior escalated. He threw the wooden chair and screamed profanity.

A young male teacher named Jim silently entered the room and stood approximately fifteen feet from Martin. Martin began screaming at Jim and repeatedly said, "I'm a big boy, you better watch out!" Carefully and calmly, Jim opened a large economics text book he was reading, thoughtfully retrieved a yellow mechanical pencil from his pocket, and began making notes in the hard-bound book. Martin screamed profanity and appeared as if he was going to attack Jim. Jim stood there silently reading. At one point, Jim looked up from his book and straight into Martin's red, screaming face. Martin, in a challenging tone, asked Jim, "You wanna go?" Meaning, "You want to fight?" Jim looked straight into Martin's eyes, said nothing, then returned to reading his book and carefully penciled a note in the margin, then turned the page.

Martin calmed and stared at his silent teacher in amazement. After fifteen minutes of reading, Jim asked Martin if he was ready for a chair. Martin nodded. Ten minutes later, Jim asked Martin if he was ready to talk about what happened. During the interview the teacher told him, "School is tough, but I'll help you to read." Martin spent the rest of the day cooling down and was brought school work. He was assigned an in-school suspension.

The next day, Martin was in tears. He explained that he was a "bad boy" who could "whip" anyone. If Jim wasn't scared of him then it meant that Jim had special karate, ninja, kung-fu, or even special forces military training, and it was unsafe to let someone with advanced combat training work with children! Martin lodged a formal complaint to the principal and to the school's resource police officer about Jim. Despite a turbulent year, Martin was able to attend the alternative school without entering state's custody. Eventually, he began reading and grew to like Jim. Martin graduated.

Learning Activity

Which of the three ingredients for building self-esteem (idealization, empathy, or belonging) best applies to this clinical vignette? Why? Please write down your answers.

2) Stop: School Setting

Albert was a sixteen-year-old intellectually challenged student in a rural school. His primary difficulty was anger. He had been expelled from his former school for violent behavior. In a rage, Albert had smashed a porcelain coffee cup on his teacher's head, seriously injuring her. He had a history of fist fighting and throwing chairs, and now attended an alternative school. Albert had an expressive language disorder that further complicated matters. The disorder made it difficult for Albert to communicate with others and he had only rudimentary verbal skills; he could ask for his basic needs, but could not engage in typical conversations. He had problems academically and struggled to read at the third-grade level.

His teachers were concerned that Albert wouldn't be able to contain his frustration. The treatment plan created by the school was simple. Albert was asked by school personnel to carry a laminated index card in his pocket with a picture of a stop sign and the word "Stop!" written in bold letters. The only expectation Albert was given at school was to "stop" if he became angry or had any uncomfortable feelings. The staff also carried "Stop!" cards. Sometimes to be playful and joke around with Albert, the staff would suddenly flash the "Stop!" card and then immediately freeze in place. Albert and some of his classmates found this very humorous. Albert's para-educator would also check in with him, giving him a thumbs-up or thumbs-down. After approximately a week of using the card, Albert appeared to forget about it and bonded with his assistant. The two of them seemed happy to eat lunch together in relative silence.

Albert attended the school for two years with no incidents of violence. He soon became well-liked by others and despite his limitations became a pro-social leader among his peers. Albert learned to work with others and built a cedar-strip canoe as a member of one of the school groups he belonged to.

Learning Activity

Which of the three ingredients for building self-esteem (idealization, empathy, or belonging) best applies to this clinical vignette? Why? Be sure to write your answers down.

3) Ronald's Reading: School Setting

> *Warning: This case study contains cruelty to animals and discrimination. It is included in an effort to contextualize a boy's academic difficulties and how he chose to belong to his family rather than learn to read.*

Ronald was tough. He lived with his father in a small cabin with dirt floors that lacked indoor plumbing. Ronald had the cognitive ability necessary for learning, but struggled with academic tasks, specifically reading. Starting from the second grade, teachers had tried multiple reading interventions. As a youngster, nothing seemed to help, and, as Ronald aged, he grew to increasingly dislike school.

Ronald became angrier and angrier. He had a piercing stare that frightened teachers. When upset, Ronald sometimes barked and growled. His behavior could be unruly and threatening; he would jump up at teachers as if to attack them. Ronald said the only thing that calmed him was tending to his birds. Tending his birds meant tormenting roosters for underground cock fighting, an illegal practice of training roosters to fight to the death. Rumor had it that Ronald and his father had a cock fighting ring. The pediatrician, protective services, and law enforcement were called. Nothing changed.

Ronald laughed that the meaner you were to a rooster, the better it fought. Much to his teachers' abhorrence, Ronald routinely bragged about hurting stray animals. As a teenager, Ronald was vocal that he disliked anyone who looked different than he did. Some days Ronald proudly wore a symbol of discrimination. Ronald refused counseling, disliked most of his teachers and peers, and could not tolerate attending class in a typical classroom. Ronald's aggressive behavior necessitated that he receive services in a small, alternative program. Ronald couldn't read or write near grade level, but in the smaller school he appeared less stressed and didn't get into fist fights.

Ronald's teachers tried to take an empathic approach with him. They tried to imagine the similarities they had with him. How were they like Ronald or his father? How could they understand his behavior as an armor shielding his vulnerabilities? Despite these attempts, faculty became resentful of Ronald. Was it fair to have to have him in their class? Why did he come to school if he just wanted to be mean? Ronald's bigotry was particularly painful for one of his teachers, despite her continued attempt to do her best to understand him, care for him, and teach him.

The school predicted that Ronald would likely drop out, so they wanted to change the focus of his education. In the morning, they wanted to continue to provide individual reading and writing instruction, and in the afternoons, they wanted to teach Ronald how to drive a commercial lawnmower. The hope was that Ronald would gain employable skills. The school feared the worst if Ronald didn't learn a trade.

To amend Ronald's educational plan, the school met with him and his father. The father was a domineering man who had a reputation for violence. Ronald's father clearly didn't support education; he rarely attended meetings at the school. Meetings generally consisted of school people telling him how troubled his son was. Ronald's father would ultimately blame the school for Ronald's problems. There seemed little possibility that the father and the school could work together.

It was difficult for the school to accept Ronald and his father. Ronald's upsetting disclosures and behaviors built an impenetrable wall of isolation. Nevertheless, the school tried its best to understand and educate Ronald.

To everyone's delight, this meeting went smoothly. The father didn't yell or threaten anyone, and thought it was good idea to learn a real skill that could help Ronald land a job. As the meeting concluded, the father told Ronald's teachers that he himself also hated school and did just fine without reading well.

Ronald's presence alone caused his teachers and principal to go on edge. None of the faculty were comfortable with the disturbing feelings that he stirred up in them. They wanted to prepare him for the future and they did, but Ronald wasn't an easy student to teach because he did little to affirm his teachers' efforts. Ronald never read at grade level, but not because of the school's lack of effort, compassion, or investment in his education. Ronald did learn how to operate and repair lawnmowers as well as other landscaping fundamentals. As expected, and against advice, Ronald quit school. But through the help of a teacher who had connections with a landscaping crew, Ronald landed an honest job.

Learning Activity

Which of the three ingredients for building self-esteem (idealization, empathy, or belonging) best applies to this clinical vignette? Why? Please write down your answers.

4) USS Limitz: School Setting

Warning: This vignette contains strong sexual material that may be upsetting to some readers. The example pertains to a high school boy who struggles with masturbation at school.

Otto was a high school student who met criteria for an Autistic Spectrum Disorder. Although he could use language, learning was tough for him, so his education focused on independent-living skills. Otto carried a collection of pyrite and other minerals with him, and in-between classes he counted them, arranged them, then carefully put them into a special, black felt bag. Otto typically minded his own business and other students generally left him alone, which was fine by him.

As Otto matured, his interest in minerals waned and was replaced with an interest in sex. Otto became obsessed with sex and began masturbating at school. Other students were very disturbed when they caught him masturbating. Further complicating matters, Otto began talking about pornography and propositioned several classmates. His classmates were repulsed; a couple of upper classmen threatened to knock him out if he even looked at their girlfriends.

Subsequently, Otto received psychotherapy. The therapist recommended that whenever Otto had an intrusive, sexual thought he should tell a trusted adult. The problem was that Otto trusted everyone. Otto graphically disclosed to his young teacher what he was thinking and made specific clothing recommendations to her. Shocked and offended, his teacher had no idea how to respond to this boy's assaultive behavior. The school suspended Otto, then explained to him the expectations. He wasn't to touch himself or talk about sex at school. This had no effect on deterring his sexualized behavior. Otto continued to masturbate at school and was now taking several bathrooms breaks a day. Rick, a kindhearted, experienced educational assistant who liked Otto, believed that Otto needed more support. Teachers, too, were increasingly concerned.

The school then consulted with a psychologist who took a different approach. The psychologist spoke with the staff and Otto's family, who was also concerned, and devised a new program for Otto. If Otto's family and faculty were willing, they would pretend that the school had transformed in to a super powerful aircraft carrier, the USS Limitz. The new plan was simple.

Otto was told that he was immediately expelled. That's it, kicked out of school forever. USS Limitz, however, gave Otto another chance. Housed in his regular school and undiscernible to the casual observer, the USS Limitz was a new experience. First, Rick was promoted to Captain and placed in absolute command of Otto. Second, maritime law governed all conduct on the USS Limitz.

Otto couldn't board the USS Limitz (his high school) until he was granted permission. Every morning, Captain Rick waited for Otto in the parking lot and stood next to a freshly painted yellow line. This line represented the USS Limitz. Otto had to ask permission to board and promise to obey all maritime law before stepping across the line and boarding ship. If Otto said that he couldn't obey the law that day, then Otto was immediately sent home. For Otto, maritime law on the USS Limitz forbade:

- Masturbation
- Pornography
- Talking about sex in any way
- Making comments regarding anyone's clothing

The USS Limitz permitted:

- Scheduled, brief bathroom breaks at the top of each hour
- Very close supervision
- A safe place he could go to if he felt overwhelmed
- Check-in conversations with Captain Rick
- Twice weekly meetings with the psychologist

Most importantly, on the USS Limitz, Otto was allowed to think any thought, have any sexual urge, and/or experience any feeling. No thought, no matter how disturbing, could hurt Otto on the USS Limitz. Thinking about sex was ok, but Otto was forbidden to do anything about it, and was only allowed to talk to the psychologist about sexual things at school.

The psychologist met with Otto to see if he liked the new plan and if he needed anything. Otto spoke with him very openly, without the natural guardedness that most people experience when talking about sex. Otto explained that he liked his new plan, was very proud to be on-board, and really liked Captain Rick. Otto immediately stopped talking about sex to his peers and teachers, and no longer masturbated at school. The psychologist explained that feelings about sex were just like other feelings. They could be talked about, understood, and used to know yourself better. The psychologist also reminded Otto that feelings weren't bad, but were private, so Otto should only talk to his psychologist, his therapist, or family about his feelings.

Over the next few weeks the school worked more closely with his therapist. The therapist increased the frequency of their meetings. It became clear that Otto suffered terribly from violent, intrusive thoughts. Otto, who was very appreciative of the school, the psychologist, and Captain Rick, worried that he wouldn't be able to control his behavior at home. Subsequently, at Otto's request, he was referred to a psychiatric treatment center for an observation and ultimately, treatment. Otto disembarked from the USS Limitz in high spirits, proud of his ability to control himself at school.

Learning Activity

Which of the three ingredients for building self-esteem (idealization, empathy, or belonging) best apply to this clinical vignette? Why? Please write down your answers.

5) No Questions: Clinical Setting

Jack was a bright twelve-year-old boy who had been referred to psychotherapy for anger problems. Jack came from an intact family with no history of trauma. He routinely entered fist fights, yelled at teachers, and displayed wild, nearly out-of-control behaviors at home and school. Jack's school wanted him in psychotherapy as a condition for attending. Jack attempted psychotherapy with a clinician, but became enraged with her during a session. Despite his parents' attempts at cajoling him into seeing his therapist again, Jack refused. When they attempted to force him into the car, Jack responded by running into the street and leaping into traffic. Thankfully, Jack wasn't hurt.

Sometime later, Jack attended therapy with a new psychologist. He went to the first two sessions peacefully, but during the third session, he refused to walk into the therapist's office building and instead ran out of the parking lot and hid in a wooded lot next to the building. Jack's father searched for his son while pleading for him to put on a coat. It was in the dead of a harsh New England winter with temperatures hovering around negative ten degrees. Jack had no gloves, hat, or jacket. The therapist joined the search.

Cold and scared, Jack begrudgingly agreed to enter the warm building on the condition that he did not have to talk. Shivering, he called the therapist "jerk face" as he walked up the stairs. Then, he folded his arms and defiantly stared at his therapist. Minutes passed as both of them thawed out. After a while, his therapist broke the silence by saying, "How terrible! I failed you." Jack replied, "I like you, but don't ask me any more questions." The therapist agreed not to ask any questions if Jack agreed to come back for another session. Jack nodded.

Sessions later, Jack explained that questions made him feel on the spot and that when the therapist asked them, it reminded him that the therapist didn't know him that well.

Learning Activity

Which of the three ingredients for building self-esteem (idealization, empathy, or belonging) best applies to this clinical vignette? Why? Be sure to write your answers down.

6) I Need a Therapist Who Gets It: Clinical Setting

Cindy, a seventeen-year-old girl, sought therapy for depression or, as she referred to it, the "Big D." As a creative artist, Cindy was terrified that her brain was defective and that she would feel awful forever. No one understood her. She felt alienated, alone, and hopeless. People, to her, were problems who required care. Cindy let no one see her vulnerabilities; instead, she cared for others.

Cindy slowly appeared to develop a sense of trust with her therapist as he attempted to empathize with her. Without medication, her depressive symptoms dissipated. She began using therapy to disclose images and dreams. Together, she and her therapist explored these dreams for meaning and playfully developed hypotheses regarding their significance. She terminated therapy when she started college. During the last session she said to her therapist, "It felt like we were sometimes the same. I know we're different, but it felt very close and at times the same. I could talk about anything with you."

Learning Activity

Which of the three ingredients for building self-esteem (idealization, empathy, or belonging) best apply to this clinical vignette? Why? Please write down your answers.

7) Gibberish: Clinical Setting

Joey was referred to treatment for ADHD. In sessions his behavior was wild. He couldn't sit still, would often spin in his chair, and vaulted over the couch. His speech was pressured. He had few friends and his mother was concerned that at ten years old, his behavior often seemed infantile.

During the first session with his therapist, Joey nearly sat in the therapist's lap. He continued attending therapy sessions with little or no improvement. In one session, Joey began speaking gibberish. His therapist responded in gibberish. For the remainder of the session and later sessions both spoke in a secret, co-created language. Following this intervention, Joey appeared much calmer. He was able to sit on the couch across from the therapist throughout the duration of the sessions. His school performance greatly improved and he made friends. Many of his ADHD symptoms disappeared.

Learning Activity

Which of the three ingredients for building self-esteem (idealization, empathy, or belonging) best applies to this clinical vignette? Why? Please write down your answers.

Learning Activities Discussion Points

1) *Ninja Teacher*

Martin needed an adult to admire whom he believed could understand and help him heal from his turbulent, emotional world. Although initially quite shaken up by Jim's cool demeanor and lack of fear about Martin's behavior, in the end this was a turning point for Martin as he found in Jim someone he could idealize. Interestingly, Martin responded very well to the school's highly structured setting, and after adopting the school's construct, relaxed his dependency on the "tough guy" persona.

2) *Stop*

Because of Albert's verbal difficulties, his assistant used non-verbal validation. He was able to empathize with Albert through his feelings and behavior. This empathic attunement helped forge the relationship that Albert needed to feel safe, settle down, and get to the hard work of learning.

3) *Ronald's Reading*

It occurred to Ronald's teachers that maybe Ronald couldn't learn to read. If he read and his father couldn't, then maybe that meant that his father couldn't be in charge. Maybe a part of Ronald unknowingly couldn't read so that he could remain emotionally close to his dad. Reading could have been too disruptive to the tenuous balance in the family. That is, Ronald's need to belong possibly trumped his desire for an education, even if that may have offered a chance at a better life. In his way, Ronald's reading difficulties were possibly a sign of allegiance to his father.

Ronald had to belong to someone. He didn't feel like he belonged at school. Teachers tried to empathize with him, but they believed he took it as weakness. He couldn't idealize his teachers because to do so may have demoted his father and toppled the hierarchy. Ronald had no choice but to belong to his father.

4) *USS Limitz*

Self-esteem enables children to control their behaviors. Although Otto had strong autistic tendencies, just like all children, he too required idealization, empathy, and belonging. This vignette doesn't explore the role that empathy or belonging did or could have played in Otto's psychotherapy treatment. Rather, it focuses on the school, providing Otto a structured environment that was strong enough to hold him and his misbehavior, and provided adults who where unafraid of him.

The intervention of pretending the school was a ship encouraged Otto to idealize both Captain Rick and the school itself. This presumably provided Otto a much needed "do over." By transforming the school into a ship, it may have communicated that Otto could also change. The aircraft carrier provided very clear limits and expectations, strengthened the school's structure, and reinforced faculty and student generational boundaries.

The intervention was designed not to overpower him, but to let him save face. Of course, if Otto didn't respond well to the intervention the school would have immediately ended it. Interestingly, Otto's school focused on idealization in an effort to curtail his behavior. Perhaps Otto could have benefited if the school had been able to take an empathic approach that was sensitive to his need to belong and understood his behavior more deeply. Most importantly, the USS Limitz didn't shame Otto.

5) No Questions

In Jack's case, the primary relational need that he desired was empathy. Jack needed his therapist to take his perspective. Questions were damaging. Jack's self-esteem was so fragile that even innocuous questions frightened him. He was communicating that he needed his therapist to merge with him.

6) I Need a Therapist Who Gets It

In a wonderful example of belonging and emotional closeness, Cindy felt deeply connected to her therapist. Through this closeness she was able to enhance her sense of self, which enabled her to move past her depressive symptoms and provided her with the courage to further her education.

7) Gibberish

Joey experienced a sense of belonging. He communicated that he felt his therapist was in the same "tribe," sharing a secret language. This like-minded experience helped Joey increase his sense of self, which ultimately helped him grow up and make friends.

Conclusion

The Healing the Self model we have explored herein is both very old and very new. It is "old" in the sense that its foundation is firmly grounded in empirical research as an evidence-based method that relies heavily on a long, studied tradition that uses existing, vetted psychotherapy approaches. On the flip side, inviting non-therapists to use this model outside of the therapeutic setting is fresh and exciting. The assumption behind the successful implementation of this model in schools is that many different adults in many different roles can and do help children grow past their anger and learn to better self-regulate. Adults can help children increase their self-esteem and thereby reduce violence in schools.

Relationships are the center of the Healing the Self model. The model is based on the fact that children develop their self-esteem through strong relationships with caring adults. Self-esteem, or a sense of self, is important because it enables people to both control their feelings and navigate the world around them. This self is developed through relationships that begin at birth. Idealization, empathy, and belonging are the core relational components required for children to develop. Without them, children behave aggressively, have excessive anger, and struggle to self-regulate. These children grow up to become emotionally fragile adults. Although *Reducing Anger and Violence in Schools* has addressed idealization, empathy, and belonging individually, it is important to remember that each of these ingredients build upon each other and are interconnected.

The first relational ingredient of the Healing the Self model, idealization, is vitally important to children because they must look up to the adult's capacity to keep them both physically and emotionally safe. Pie's story in Chapter 2 is the perfect illustration of why kids need adult role models. Pie was angry because he didn't feel he had anyone he could look up to, but when he allowed himself to admire Rob's rock climbing abilities and was entrusted with learning those skills by Rob, Pie began to believe in parts of himself. When a child admires someone who then likes the child, the process allows the child to see himself as worthy and good.

Empathy, the second relational ingredient in the model, is required to understand someone else's perspective or, as they say, "walk in their shoes," and is fundamental to a child's healthy development. Everyone is at their best when they're understood. Sam, who was highlighted in Chapter 9, was furious with his sister and it wasn't until his therapist tried to understand his perspective that Sam could move past his frustration. Frustration, anger, and rage result when someone important to a child fails empathically, or in other words, fails to understand why something is desperately important to a child. Anger is secondary to disappointment or empathic failures. Empathy extinguishes anger.

The third relational ingredient, belonging, is a basic human need that children must feel from infancy in order to fully develop. When a child feels wanted and has the sense that they belong, they feel safe enough to lower their guard and increase their vulnerability. When Jamie, whose story was highlighted in Chapter 3, felt like she and Helen were together, she developed a sense of belonging with her teacher and perhaps this sense enabled her to stop hitting other students. Belonging is created through authentic closeness and vulnerability. True belonging is forged through experiences that demonstrate our flaws, short-comings, and vulnerabilities. Children belong to others only after they are truly known for their difficulties and their successes, and adults feel these feelings with them.

Although Healing the Self is a model of development that greatly prioritizes the self, it's just one of many approaches that can help children mature. It should not be considered a comprehensive model of the mind nor a complete approach to helping all children grow in all ways. Rather, it merely outlines important relational ingredients that, if applied thoughtfully and individually, will, with luck, have the power to build the relationships children need to overcome anxiety and frustration.

We then outlined how the model fits within the tradition of evidence-based practices, as well as special considerations regarding how the model can be applied in the school, home, and of course, the therapy office. Each chapter included a case study illustrating salient points. Perhaps noticeably, the one group of people not given a chapter are the teachers, therapists, and others who use this model. One might ask, what are the consequences for the adults using the Healing the Self method?

Grant, like so many other children, became better able to handle the bumps and bruises of everyday life. He no longer lost it. But his teacher, Melanie, changed, too. She grew to understand that just as Grant's "fishing" wasn't about catching fish, she also had ways of camouflaging disappointments. Melanie grew to think more deeply about her students, her coworkers, family, and herself. By permitting herself to care more deeply and more thoughtfully for others, her life improved. Working this way didn't drain her, it renewed her enthusiasm for teaching. Most importantly, thinking symbolically enabled her to better understand herself and her family.

Melanie is not alone. Teachers, educational assistants, school counselors, therapists, parents, pediatricians, and others who have used the model have remarked that not only does it help children, but it sparked curiosity regarding their own relationships and themselves. That perhaps they, too, engaged in the world to sometimes protect themselves from powerful feelings while reaching out to others, and that that's "ok." That thinking deeply about others inevitably causes one to think deeply about themselves. Moreover, an educational assistant disclosed that a windfall to this model was that by thinking about student relationship needs, teachers became aware of each other's needs, and that the faculty became closer. When we think about people, in this way, even the adults get along better.

Change is complex and can take on many different forms. In addition, lasting change takes time. Although the Healing the Self approach equips adults with a new way of thinking about and understanding relationships, working with children is tough. Determining the difference between our self-esteem needs and our students' needs is a lifelong process. Although the basic ingredients—idealization, empathy, and belonging—may appear simple, providing them can be difficult. Anyone who works with children knows that offering them what they need, even with a clear game-plan in an ideal setting and with a strong team, is still a very challenging task.

Finally, no matter how dedicated, professional, or thoughtful the teacher or therapist is, sometimes, children do not get better. Every teacher or child therapist has worked with a child in a situation that didn't go as planned. No one person can help everyone. But as teachers, therapists, and parents, we have to remind ourselves that helping children is inherently good and that doing good, despite not being able to see a positive outcome, is a worthy pursuit.

Even though teaching and helping children can be challenging, the Healing the Self model opens up new possibilities for understanding, comforting, soothing, and strengthening children. Healing the Self invites adults to reconsider the relationship they have with the children with whom they work, because it's the relationship itself that provides the intervention that can help reduce aggression and anger while increasing self-regulation. The model is an invitation for adults to ponder concepts and consider if these concepts can be applied to others and to their own childhood. Too often in schools, developmental models of psychological change consist of asking adults to "Do more!" which may further stress or shame teachers or others in school systems that are already at maximum capacity. At its core, Healing the Self suggests that adults thinking about their relationships with children can be curative. The most important lesson taught through Healing the Self is that it's the relationship that counts. Melanie, like all the adults in this book, helped the struggling student, not by what she did, but by being there. In the end, it was the relationship.

Glossary of Terms

Affect: The outside expression of a feeling. For example, smiling.

Aggression: Often resulting from anger, it, too, is an attempt to feel whole. Aggression stems from disappointments.

Anger: Often a reaction to feeling misunderstood; it can be an attempt to feel whole.

Anger/Violence/Self-Esteem Trio: For many children, anger turns to violence. This is because they haven't yet developed strong self-esteem, which both reduces anger and enables children to control their emotions and behaviors.

Assertiveness: May look similar to aggression but comes from excitement, joy, and positive energy.

Authenticity: Children with low self-esteem need adults to be real so they can admire the adult.

Behavior: Something that can be seen on the outside. For instance, Johnny was angry so he punched Jimmy. Punching is the behavior; anger is the feeling.

Belonging: Feeling connected to someone or a group. This is a basic need people have, and when it's met, they're at their best.

Compliments: Children with low self-esteem can't take compliments.

Defensiveness: People are defensive when they fear they will be misunderstood; an attempt to be less vulnerable.

Emotional Closeness: An experience of feeling deeply understood by another. It is very difficult to put into words because it mimics what infants feel before they develop language.

Empathic Failure: When a child wishes an adult understood him or her better; it alone can be traumatizing.

Empathy: Taking someone else's perspective. This requires feeling, thinking, sensing, and imagining another's point of view.

Empirical Support: Unbiased scientific research that transcends personal opinion and relies on a specific method of inquiry.

Evidence-based Practice: A practice (medical or educational) that is grounded in good judgment, patient/student preferences, and empirical support.

Generational Boundaries: The many differences between adults and children. Convincing children that they are adults robs them of their childhood and the ability to mature into functioning adults when they grow older.

Idealization: Children naturally admire adults' capacity to care for them. Children must idealize others before they can believe in themselves.

Imagination: Children live in the world of pretend.

Like-minded: When someone feels very similar to another.

Meta-analysis: Examining multiple scientific studies to gain a clear picture of something.

Mirroring: When an adult matches a child's expression, such as smiling back at a child.

Patient: Someone suffering.

Psychodynamic Therapy: A highly effective, depth-oriented form of talk therapy that prioritizes the therapist-patient relationship.

Self-esteem: The core of someone's personality. Self-esteem enables children to feel rather than "do" emotions. It's created through relationships with adults that include idealization, empathy, and a sense of belonging.

Self-regulation: Children's self-esteem enables them to self-regulate, i.e., to control both their feelings and behaviors.

Sense of Self: Expanded self-esteem; it includes how people treat others.

Structuring: Providing clear limits and expectations to foster healthy idealization.

Transference: When someone treats the therapist as if he or she is someone else.

Unmet Belonging: Children with low self-esteem may get their belonging needs met by engaging in destructive relationships.

Unmet Empathic Needs: When children haven't had their empathic needs met they may have difficulty developing their identity; have a deep sense of inadequacy; and/or have difficulties determining reality.

Unmet Idealization: When children can't idealize adults they often believe their own emotions can't be controlled. They may grow up to be show-offs or need to be fancier than others to compensate for deep feelings of inadequacy.

Validation: Shows empathy; it can be done through behavior, feelings, and words.

Validation Through Affect: Sharing an emotion with a child with words and/or actions.

Validation Through Words: Guessing the child's experience and saying it. For instance, asking a child if they are mad when they appear angry.

Violence: An attempt to feel whole by forcing others to take the attacker's perspective and idealize him or her. Violence indicates low self-esteem.

Index